FOXES
UNEARTHED

FOXES
UNEARTHED

A STORY OF LOVE AND LOATHING
IN MODERN BRITAIN

LUCY JONES

This paperback edition first published in 2017

ISBN: 978-1-78396-304-1

With thanks to the Roald Dahl Literary Estate for permission to quote
from material from the Roald Dahl Museum and Story Centre's archives.
Roald Dahl's book *Fantastic Mr Fox* is published by Puffin Books.

9 8 7 6 5 4 3 2 1

A catalogue record for this book is available from the British Library.

Cover illustration by Nathan Burton
Interior illustrations by Tim Oakenfull
Typesetting by Marie Doherty
Printed by CPI Group (UK) Ltd, Croydon, CR0 4YY

Contents

Prologue

Of all the mammals in Britain, it is the fox that has cast its spell on me. I find it, as one of the largest predators left in our islands, a captivating creature: a comfortably familiar figure in our country landscapes; an intriguing flash of bright-eyed wildness in our towns.

It is an animal that is often surrounded by myth and controversy, and my own experiences of the fox have proved just as complicated and conflicting. Traditionally, one side of my family had a fondness for hunting – particularly my late grandfather, whom I adored, admired and respected. In my early years, fox hunting was an accepted part of life. It was only as I grew older, and my own partiality for the fox began to emerge, that I started to question the activity. The fox, in my experience, has always been more than just a wild animal. He is a character, an emblem, a flint for emotions and ethical questions; in short, he poses something of a quandary for us here in Britain, in both town and country.

As a reluctant city-dweller, I'm no stranger to glimpsing foxes on our streets – as townies we may not have otters or hares or ptarmigans or capercaillies, but we do have *Vulpes vulpes* in abundance. It had been a while since I'd spotted one, though, and I decided to walk through Walthamstow Marshes in London, the nearest large green space to my home, to see the animal in action. The area is a biodiversity hotspot, home to flowers, plants, insects and voles. Two pairs of kestrels had moved in, and they hovered and dived like feathered meteors into the marshlands.

To up my chances, I turned to *Fox Watching* by Martin Hemmington, a practical guide for would-be ecologists. First, keep eyes and nose peeled for hair, droppings, paw prints and the smell of urine. Second, wear camouflage clothes with black or brown shoes. Third, bring binoculars, writing equipment and dinner. Fourth, patience is essential. I left the house before dusk armed with new knowledge and a slice of spinach pie in my pocket. As the air cooled, the scent of the marshes intensified. Large slugs with patterned backs slithered in scores across the path – food for foxes, if they fancied it. The lights of a train lit up the trail as I walked into the undergrowth, looking for vulpine scat and hoping a fox would cross my path.

As it turns out, though, foxes can be elusive creatures when you're in active pursuit, and my search proved frustratingly fruitless that night, as did many that followed. For some reason, our paths were just not crossing. I was beginning to think the fox population in our cities was being grossly exaggerated.

When I finally did stumble across a fox, it was completely by accident. I was ambling home through busy, built-up Stoke Newington, my mind elsewhere, certainly not on foxes. And suddenly, there it was. It emerged gingerly at first, peeking through the railings of a railway bridge. Standing on the pavement by a busy crossroads at around eight o'clock in the evening, close to shops, restaurants, pubs and houses, it waited for the traffic to clear, its head turning back and forth, eyes following the cars, ears pricked. Its brush was long, full and rich, slightly darker than the rest of its pelage, and turned up at the end at a jaunty angle. It crowned a long, lithe body, its wintry fur coat a rusty, burnt ochre. The fur on its throat was white, giving the impression it was wearing a bib. We made eye contact; it looked intelligent, curious, for the most part nonchalant. Its eyes were an amber gold, lit up by the headlights, expressionless and cool. Around the muzzle and those sharp teeth, the fur was white. I wanted to get closer but, wary of spooking it, hung back to keep it in my sight as long as possible. It soon trotted off and vanished through the gate of an apartment complex.

Even though I'd seen lots of foxes over the decade I'd lived in London, I experienced a jolt; a pure, chemical thrill. Various associations rushed through my head – memories of taxidermied fox heads in my grandparents' house, *Fantastic Mr Fox*, the vulpine 'psycho' killer of a recent news report, Ted Hughes's bold and brilliant Thought-Fox – and I felt excitement, wonder, surprise. Yet I knew my reaction wouldn't have been universal.

When you see a fox, what do you feel? More than any other animal in Britain, the fox can elicit a cocktail of opinion and emotion. It is rarely a blank canvas. Perhaps you see the fox as vermin, a pest to be shot as quickly as possible, a rude interloper who doesn't belong in the human space. Perhaps you see a beautiful wild animal or a cute pet to be fed. Or perhaps you see a cunning rogue waiting to be hunted. You might feel annoyed if a fox once killed your chickens or your pet tortoise. You might feel elated to witness the largest British carnivore so casually on a street corner. You might even feel a little frightened, a natural response to coming face to face with what is still a wild animal.

In his book *Arctic Dreams*, Barry Lopez remarked vividly on the sensation of human–animal collision. 'Few things provoke like the presence of wild animals. They pull at us like tidal currents with questions of volition, of ethical involvement, of ancestry,' he wrote. The currents that exist around the fox in Britain are powerful, old and complex.

They have combined to create an enigmatic character, rarely perceived for what it actually is.

The fox has come to represent a thorny and emotive array of concepts to different people: from liberty to beauty, class to cruelty, hunter to hunted, pin-up to pest. In no other culture but Britain's is the animal so polarising and so complex a public figure, perceived ambiguously by its human neighbours, on both a local level and in national debate. No other creature in Britain has provoked or inspired more column inches, literary characters, pop-culture symbols, parliamentary hours, lyrics, album covers, cartoons, nicknames, pub names, jewellery, tea coasters, cushion covers, Facebook fights, hashtags, demonstrations, rallies, words and sheer cortisol than the fox. Former prime minister Tony Blair described the passions aroused by fox hunting as 'primeval'. 'If I'd proposed solving the pension problem by compulsory euthanasia for every fifth pensioner I'd have got less trouble,' he wrote in his memoirs about the row over Labour's Hunting Act, which banned hunting wild mammals with dogs.

The conflicting emotions – passionate love and hate – that the fox inspires is a fascinating phenomenon. To understand fully how attitudes, experiences and agendas collided to create this peculiar variation in our feelings towards *Vulpes vulpes*, we must delve into the history of the fox in Britain and how our relationship with this wily mammal has evolved over millennia.

As Cunning as a Fox

The cerulean sky set everything off the day I travelled to Great Missenden, the little country village in the Chilterns made famous by its erstwhile resident Roald Dahl, to visit his archives. Trees were slightly burnished by the beginning of autumn and leaves browned like the top of an apple crumble. The houses became quaint and pretty as the train whizzed out of London.

Dahl was born in Cardiff in 1916 to Norwegian parents. He started writing during the Second World War and, in 1943, *The Gremlins* was published, the first of a run of funny and imaginative stories published in hundreds of languages. Unlike other children's books, Dahl's writing was never didactic or moralising; he revelled in high jinks and naughtiness. 'I am passionately obsessed with making the young readers laugh and squirm and love the story. They know it's not true. They know from the start it's a fairy tale, so the content is never going to influence their minds one way or another,' he once said.

The author's writing hut has been replicated exactly in the Roald Dahl Museum and Story Centre. His ashtray, complete with cigarette butts, sat on the makeshift desk that rests on an armchair made specially to accommodate his back problems. Spectacles and other personal items were nearby: family photos, drawings, trinkets, lighters, mementoes. The lino is as it was: blue, red and yellow diamonds on a green background. It's the same lino filmmaker Wes Anderson gave to the study floor of his Mr Fox in the popular film based on the book. Dahl sat in his hut from ten in the morning until twelve, even when stuck, to write. 'It is my little nest, my womb,' he said. From there he could see down to an ancient beech called the Witches' Tree – the very one where he imagined a certain Mr Fox and his family lived.

The most famous fox in British literature today emerged in 1970. Dahl's Fantastic Mr Fox was a complete transformation in the way foxes are perceived in this country – traditionally seen as a wicked trickster, he now became the first unequivocal fox hero. The very fact that a new vision of the fox had appeared provides fascinating insights into the tensions around the fox's place in Britain.

The plot of *Fantastic Mr Fox* sees our hero as a predator to be admired. With the fox family being relentlessly hunted by three nasty farmers, Mr Fox comes up with the idea of taking food from each of their farms through a series of underground tunnels. He gathers a vast feast for all the other families trapped by the farmers' determination to kill the crafty fox, and for that he is dubbed fantastic. Dahl created characters and a plot that make us delight, cheer and punch the air when the foxes outfox the repulsive farmers and feast on livestock and poultry to their hearts' content.

In the archives I discovered that the first draft was different from the story we know today. The foxes – and Dahl's original drawings of them are charming – dig up into the Main Street supermarket and fill their trolleys with cake and eggs and pie and candy and toys. Mr Fox is still the provider, but the family is essentially stealing from faceless shopkeepers. 'The cops are still looking for the robbers,' reads the final line.

The American publishers were concerned that this 'glorification of theft', as Roald Dahl's biographer Donald Sturrock put it, would put off libraries and schoolteachers from promoting the book. Editor Fabio Coen wrote to Dahl with a suggestion. Instead of stealing from the supermarkets, the foxes should steal from the horrible farmers. 'It would also hold something of a moral,' he wrote. 'Namely that you cannot prevent others from securing sustenance without yourself paying a penalty.' Dahl was thrilled with his editor's ingenuity. 'I'll grab them with both hands and get to work at once on an entirely new version,' he wrote. Later, there were conversations about whether the fox really needed to kill the three chickens in the coop, and a suggestion was made that the fox should just collect a huge basket of eggs instead. Dahl insisted that this would not be right.

'Foxes are foxes and as you're right to say they are killers,' he explained. The decision was made that it wouldn't distress children and the foxes' natural activity was kept in. Fox is a hero in spite of his natural carnivorous behaviour. He is cunning, and he is celebrated for it.

I wandered to the field near Gipsy House, where Dahl and his family once lived, to see the beech trees under which the real Mr Fox built his den. Hedgerows covered in clots of red hawthorn berries and blackberries the colour of dried blood bordered the footpath. Summer was over and the honeysuckle looked ropey. The late-afternoon September light made the foliage glow green and dappled the damp forest floor. It was quiet and seemed a fitting place for a fox family to make its home.

Dahl would have been well aware as he was writing that he had chosen an animal whose image was starting to be fiercely contested, that perhaps it was now ready for a more sympathetic portrayal. Although he never spoke publicly about fox hunting during his life, when he was sixteen and boarding at Repton School in the Midlands, he wrote an essay about hunting. The archivist at the Roald Dahl Museum dug it out during my visit. It is a forcible argument for why Dahl believed hunting to be 'foolish, pointless and cruel'. He concedes that riding a horse is enjoyable but questions the need to have 'something to chase, something at which to shout and blow trumpets . . . and finally to satisfy their bloodthirsty minds'. The red fox is described as 'small', 'valiant' and 'little'; he 'tires' and 'takes shelter'. Dahl recounts what happens if the animal is found: 'Slaughter takes place, after which certain young and usually too well-nourished members step forward to have the blood of sacrifice smeared on their faces.' Dahl's visceral and imaginative wit shows early: the huntsman has the appearance of 'having been grown in the dark'.

Dahl then draws a comparison between the killing of the fox and the lady who cries when her Pekinese gets a thorn in its paw. It is 'incredible', he writes, that the same lady should gloat at a fox being 'torn to pieces'. The piece ends with the assertion that the most humane method of killing foxes is surely to shoot them. Although views do, of course, change, it is still an interesting insight. We know Dahl was an animal-lover: he owned dogs, cats, goats and even 200 budgerigars at one point, and in his book *The Magic Finger*, published in 1966, a young girl who abhors hunting uses her magic to turn a local hunting family into the ducks they shoot.

Compare Dahl's portrayal of the fox, a noble and sympathetic creature, with another: licking his lips, eyes narrowed and thickly kohled beneath comic, angry eyebrows, often surrounded by a cloud of feathers, the fox is unequivocally dangerous, but also clever, and therefore a worthy opponent for sport. He even has a name: Charlie. This is the fox of the nineteenth and twentieth centuries, and if you read the classic hunting literature, you'd believe this fox is more attractive than the average town fox you might see today: richer in hue, it could be mistaken for a flame if you caught a glimpse of it across a field. He was distinguished from other animals by his cunning – he could roll in manure so that the hounds would lose his scent or run across bridges or swim across lakes. In a way, he was master of his own destiny. Some sources even suggested Charlie enjoyed being hunted, looking back at the hounds with a smile and a chuckle.

When I see a fox, I'm aware that I am utterly influenced by the stories I've been told, the pictures I've absorbed, the rumours I've heard. Foxes have a rich history in this country, as a creature we have used for our own physical needs, as fur, food or medicine, but also as one that has captured our collective imagination, at various times a rogue, a villain, a trickster, a character to be admired or reviled.

But what, fundamentally, is the fox? Above all, it is a brilliant opportunist, capable of exploiting a huge range of ecological habitats and environments, and this is one of the reasons why it is so widespread around the world. It has colonised most of the northern hemisphere with a greater geographical range and concentration than any other carnivore on earth. Altogether, there are twelve distinct species of fox, each adapted to its environment, from the tiny, delightfully big-eared fennec (*Vulpes zerda*) of the Sahara desert to the snow-white, fluffy-bodied Arctic fox (*Vulpes lagopus*), found in colder climates such as Iceland. But it is the red fox that is indigenous to Britain.

The most instantly striking characteristic of this animal is its colour. The red fox is, as its name suggests, a vivid, bright shade of reddish orange, a startlingly eye-catching hue that varies in intensity from pale apricot via ruddy red to the fiery orange of volcanic lava. The fur on the neck and chest is softer, fluffy and white as is, usually, the bob on the end of the brush. Its legs, brush and the hairs on its ears will also be tinted with black. Occasionally 'black' red foxes have been spotted, as the amount of darker fur varies from animal to animal. The red fox is long, thin and surprisingly small, on average only between 46 and 86 centimetres long, excluding the tail which can be another 30 to 55 centimetres.

The face of a fox is mesmerising – handsome, even. The ears are prominent, triangular, adorable, with soft black or white hair tufts inside. The eyes are an extraordinary gold colour, quite light and shaped like a cat's, and its expression is naturally alert, conscious – even clever, especially when it narrows its eyes.

Animals cannot speak and so we speak for them. Across Europe, one of the enduring perceptions of the fox lies in the idea of vulpine intelligence. It has existed for centuries, millennia even, and has been one of the animal's defining characteristics, from the human point of view, although with varying interpretations and ramifications over the years.

More than 2,500 years ago, in Ancient Greece, a slave called Aesop created what would become a long-enduring representation of the fox. Aesop supposedly came up with hundreds of fables, which were short and to the point, sometimes just a couple of sentences long, mostly about animals, and often including a moral lesson about human behaviour. For a number of them, his authorship is debatable: some have roots in Indian, Talmud and various folkloric traditions. In any case, the fox is a recurring character in his stories, and a clear picture of the fox's characteristics quickly appears.

In one tale, the fox leads the newly crowned king ape to a baited trap; the ape accuses him of treachery. In another, a crow has found a piece of cheese and retires to a branch to eat it; the fox flatters her by asking if her voice is as beautiful as her looks; the bird sings and drops the cheese into the fox's mouth. A lion is pretending to be sick to lure animals into his cave; the fox hangs back – he can see paw prints only going in, not coming out; he survives. A lion and a bear fight each other for a young fawn; the fox waits until they fall asleep from exhaustion and sneaks in to snaffle their prey. A fox enters the hollow of a tree to eat food left there by a shepherd; he eats so much, he is too fat to escape. A fox tries to reach grapes but he's not tall enough. A fox tries to eat soup from a stork's bowl but it's too narrow.

Aesop's stories reveal a couple of common threads. First, the fox was perceived to have an appetite, and he is prepared to step into other animals' spaces to get a meal. Second, he is able to get this food through trickery. He can think ahead and use his wits to protect himself. And, crafty and elusive, he is often successful. The fox's wits are referred to using the Greek word *poikilos*, which means something difficult to define, varied, manifold, of different colours and shades. A shape-shifter, in a way. The fox, according to the earliest fables, was smart.

It is worth taking a moment to examine what is understood by 'intelligence' in a fox, and whether there is truth to the reputation that the fox is cleverer than other animals. Canids have high levels of cognitive ability, as many social animals do. The fox is an adept hunter, successfully resourceful, opportunistic and adaptable to different environments. Evolutionary pressure has made the species adept at assessing and exploiting availability. 'The fox can make decisions quickly and solve problems to get food,' explained Dr Dawn Scott of the University of Brighton, who has studied canids for decades, and the red fox in particular. 'That ability to exploit and adapt means that natural selection has driven it to be able to solve problems. And that's how we assess intelligence: ability to solve problems.'

There are certainly examples of what we might consider clever behaviour. Aelian, the Roman author writing around 200 AD, gives an early account of a fox's ability to trick. A fox could sneak up on a bustard, a large terrestrial bird common on the steppes of the Old World, by raising its tail and pressing the front of its body to the ground, it could artfully change itself into a persuasive silhouette of the bird.

One of the most famous tactics the fox is said to deploy is that of playing dead, either to escape capture or to outwit prey, and there have been many examples of this in literature and art over the centuries. The *Physiologus*, a second-century Christian text, tells of the fox feigning death: 'When he is hungry and nothing turns up for him to devour, he rolls himself in red mud so that he looks as if he were stained with blood. Then he throws himself on the ground and holds his breath, so that he positively does not seem to breathe. The birds, seeing that he is not breathing, and that he looks as if he were covered with blood with his tongue hanging out, think that he is dead and come down to sit on him. Well, thus he grabs them and gobbles them up.'

In January 2016 the ruse was actually caught on film. Siberian hunters came across what appeared to be a dead Arctic fox, trapped in one of their snares. The video shows the fox being manhandled as they remove the snare; it never flinches, its eyes remain closed and face motionless. It looks utterly dead. But almost as soon as the men place the body in a cardboard box, the fox bursts out, leaps high into the air and scrambles across the snow for its life, soon to be joined by a group of Arctic fox pals. It is a stunning sequence of supposed thought, ingenuity and wits.

Another folkloric tale of the fox's intelligence is that the fox, if troubled by fleas, takes a piece of wool in his mouth and trots to the nearest river for a cooling swim. The fleas, desperate to avoid drowning in the water, congregate on the strip of wool. Once they're all in one place, the fox releases the wool into the river, thus getting rid of his unwelcome guests. It is a common tale in different parts of the world and we don't know the exact origin: it was popular in Celtic communities but there's a similar version about a jackal in India. Even though it's unlikely to be true, the tale still exists today; it was recounted to me as fact by a man in the Lake District in 2015.

Partly as a result of its supposed intelligence, the fox has often been seen as a threat to human interests. While it would not have been in direct competition with humans for food in the remote past, a major change for the fox, and for other wild mammals, occurred when domestic livestock was introduced – in Britain, the earliest sheep are dated to over 5,000 years ago.

The fox had been around for many thousands of years – the oldest fox remains in Britain date back to the Wolstonian period (between 130,000 and 352,000 years ago) from Tornewton Cave in South Devon. Remains of wolf, lion, badger, bear, horse, reindeer, clawless otter, rhino and bison were also found in the same stratum so we can imagine a countryside teeming with mammals of all shapes and sizes, alongside the fox. With other such predators around, the fox would have found itself in competition for food, and it would even occasionally have become prey to an opportunistic bear, wolf or lion. But it also would have posed only a secondary threat to humans.

As the ice sheets melted at the end of Europe's final glaciation, around 12,000 years ago, vegetation gradually became more abundant across Britain as the land began to blossom into a scene more familiar to us now, allowing the wildlife, including foxes, to flourish.

But it was with the shift to a farming culture that foxes started to cause a problem for human settlements. An animal with an omnivorous diet, the fox would have been partial to a grape or two, so in direct competition with early farmers for the food they were cultivating, as well as to their livestock.

At first, the fox might have benefited from its new

barnyard neighbours. It was much easier for people to eat their domestic animals than go hunting with snares, traps or spears, and the fox wasn't as much of a threat to sheep, cattle, goats and pigs as were bears and wolves. While the bigger mammals were still roaming the countryside, the fox could keep a low profile, even though its population was widespread across Britain.

The earliest and clearest account of the fox troubling livestock is from Pliny the Elder. A Roman naturalist and scholar writing in the first century AD, he suggested practical methods for farmers to keep foxes at bay. One simple solution, for example, was to feed chickens the fried liver of a fox, which would prevent them from being attacked. A slightly more complicated way of protecting one's hen involved cutting a collar of skin from the neck of the fox and affixing it to a cockerel's neck. The hens that mated with the cock thus adorned were immune from being hunted and killed by the local fox. Presumably there is some logic to this: foxes are territorial and mark their territories with scent from their various glands. Foxes observed in areas of Britain by the eminent Scottish biologist and zoologist Professor David Macdonald of Oxford University would very rarely cross boundaries laid down by another fox group even if food was available. A fox might have been so put off by the smell of the makeshift necklace that the poultry was given wide berth.

Fear and apparent threats to human lives or settlements – such as wild animals – are powerful. They have a way of gripping our collective imagination, entering our storytelling traditions and gradually becoming increasingly magnified to the point where they can transform into an enemy of mythic proportions.

And the fox is indeed presented as menacing in early European myths and stories. In Greek mythology, for example, the Teumessian fox, also known as the Cadmean vixen, was an enormous fox that could never be caught. The vixen, which had been sent by the gods as punishment for an unrecorded crime, plagued the population of Thebes by eating people's babies. Eventually, the beast was stopped when the dog Laelaps, who could always catch its prey, was brought in to pursue the fox. Faced with an impossible paradox, Zeus turned both creatures into stone and flung them into the skies – where they remain to this day as the constellations Canis major and Canis minor.*

---

* Canis major is not the only fox in our skies. In the northern skies, there is a faint constellation that was discovered in the seventeenth century by Johannes Hevelius. He originally called it Vulpecula et Anser, meaning 'little fox and goose', and he depicted it as a fox carrying a goose in its jaws. These days it is just known as Vulpecula, although the brightest star is called Anser in reference to the goose.

The fox's perceived intelligence, when exercised in competition for food, might be interpreted as devious rather than smart. Between admiration for that cunning and dislike for the fox's thieving tendencies, the ambiguous relationship humans have developed with the fox emerged fully in the popular culture of the Middle Ages. The hugely popular and influential stories of Reynard the Fox acknowledged his sneaky habits, but also seem to display a grudging respect and admiration for the animal.

It is unclear who invented the character of Reynard, but versions of the story were certainly popular around Europe. In the preface to German writer Johann Wolfgang von Goethe's epic poem *Reineke Fuchs* (1794), he suggests that the first account was by Nivardus, a Flemish ecclesiastic attached to the monastery of St Peter at Ghent in 1148. Different accounts of Reynard spread through Europe, following Pierre de Saint-Cloud's *Roman de Renart* during the thirteenth and fourteenth centuries with *Die Hystorie van Reynaert die Vos* published in Dutch in 1479, from which William Caxton took his first English translation of 1481. In an early illumination from the manuscript of *Roman de Renart*, in the thirteenth century, a fox sits upright on a horse, wearing armour and an orange cape. His eyes look slightly upwards as he plunges his sword into the heart of Ysengrim the wolf. In another image from later in the same century, a large fox, with a goose in its mouth, leaps away from a woman. The goose's head flops out of the fox's jaws; his claws look sharp and dangerous. You can almost see the bubbling white saliva dripping from his teeth. The eyes are narrowed and elongated, seeming to denote wickedness.

The general plot of *Reynard* is quite simple. It begins in the court of King Noble, a lion, where locals have turned up to complain about Reynard's anti-social behaviour. He blinded my cubs, says Isegrim the wolf. He nicked my pudding, says Courtuys the dog. He ate my chicks, weeps Chanticleer the cock. The King summons Bruin the bear to bring Reynard in. Reynard agrees to go with Bruin to court, but, before they leave, he wonders whether the bear might like a taste of honey? Bruin sticks his head in a log, where it gets stuck, and rips off half his face and his ears trying to get free. Reynard 1, King 0. Then, Tybalt the cat is sent to get Reynard. He returns with one eye. Reynard 2, King 0.

Reynard eventually relents and goes to the King, and the rest of the story is a dialogue between the two in which Reynard's dirty work is discovered but wriggled out of with an imaginative lie. He succeeds by outwitting the other animals with cunning tricks that play on their weaknesses. He bullies, he kills, he wins.

Reynard was a bestseller in the Middle Ages and has been rewritten and translated a number of times since. Its popularity may have been due to it fulfilling a need: medieval beast fables were usually not about animals, but about humans and human relations, using animal characters to satirise human society as well as personifying certain traits and emotions. As Joan Acocella wrote in a *New Yorker* essay, 'Animals are fun – they have feathers and fangs, they live in trees and holes – and they seem to us simpler than we are, so that, by using them, we can make our points cleaner and faster.' Creating a story around animal characters engaged people, while also carrying a moral or deeper meaning.

The character has gone on to inspire tales in different art forms, from Stravinsky's opera-ballet *Renard* to Ben Jonson's *Volpone*, from the stories of Chicken Licken to Janáček's *Cunning Little Vixen*. In the nineteenth century Reynard was the basis for the ballad of Reynardine, a werefox who lured beautiful women to his castle, to an undisclosed fate. He's even been immortalised in British hunting songs – and, indeed, 'Reynard' is still a name for a male fox in the UK:

> *On the first day of Spring in the year ninety-three*
> *the first recreation was in this country,*
> *the King's County gentleman o'er hills, dales and rocks,*
> *they rode out so jovially in search of a fox.*

> *Chorus: Tally-ho, hark away, tally-ho, hark away,*
> *tally ho, hark away, boys, away.*

> *When Reynard first started he faced Tullamore,*

Arklow and Wicklow along the seashore,
he kept his brush in view every yard of the way,
and it's straight he took his course through the streets of Roscrea.

Chorus

But Reynard, sly Reynard, he lay hid that night,
they swore they would watch him until the daylight,
early the next morning the woods they did resound,
with the echo of horns and the sweet cry of hounds.

Chorus

When Reynard was started he faced to the hollow,
where none but the hounds and footmen could follow,
the gentlemen cried: 'Watch him, watch him, what shall we do?
If he makes it to the rocks then he will cross Killatoe!'

Chorus

Bur Reynard, sly Reynard, away he did run,
away from the huntsman, away from the gun,
the gentleman cried: 'Home, boys, there's nothing we can do,
for Reynard is away and our hunting is through.'

Chorus

In 2014, the first series of *Bosch*, a noir detective TV drama set in Los Angeles, had as its villain one 'Raynard Waits', a pseudonym devised by the character. Michael Connelly, from whose novel the TV show was adapted, made his Raynard crafty and apt to change his appearance, a direct reference to the character traits of the Flemish tale. Both have the same raison d'être: to prey and outwit. Waits, now on the run, calls Bosch (King Lion) to confess, to trick, to wind up, delighting in the fact he has one up on the police as he goes around murdering prostitutes and adding to his skull shrine. Reynard lives on in human form.

Mostly, Reynard is a villain we cheer for. The Caxton translation is written with a delight at the character's Machiavellian quality: we enjoy watching the play of intelligence in contrast with the stupidity and gullibility of the other animals. It is inconsistent, though. On the one hand, the reader is invited to enjoy Reynard's outrageous lies and one-upmanship over his boorish peers. 'An ass is an ass,' says Reynard. 'Yet many have risen in the world. What a pity.' And we can't help but agree. On the other, his activity is violent: he rapes the wolf's wife and causes many a gory injury. Caxton, towards the end of the epic, warns against such behaviour and suggests we weed out character defects similar to the ones the fox displays. Yet, it all ends happily ever after for Reynard, which suggests he is, if not the hero, at least an anti-hero. He is charismatic, and, to use Colin Willock's phrase, 'splendidly nefarious'.

Reynard was not the only fox story of the times. Chaucer wrote a cunning fox, Russell, into his *Canterbury Tales*. His was a retelling of Aesop's 'The Fox and the Crow', which further popularised the story in Britain. This was in the 1390s, when Britain was experiencing harsh weather, with savage winters and wet summers, which would have put increasing pressure on food production, and people were badly malnourished. The country was also still recovering from the Black Death epidemic in 1348, which had wiped out half of the population. Any predatory mammal would have been seen as a threat to human sustenance. It was at this time that Chaucer's Russell, in the Nun's Priest's Tale, is 'full of sly iniquity' and lurks in a bed of cabbage with the intention of taking Chanticleer the rooster. He manages to make off with the bird after convincing him to close his eyes and sing, although the rooster escapes in the end.

In a practical sense, tales about pilfering foxes gave instruction to farmers about protecting their livestock. But the fox had also become a clear symbol for a variety of moral failings. As most people were illiterate, such a message could be communicated quickly an clearly through imagery, which more often than not would be conveyed through the Church, the main source of information for many.

The Church already had a long history of portraying

the fox as a villain, going back to early descriptions in the Bible. It appears as a thief: the author of Song of Songs, thought to have been written around 200 BC, accuses the fox of ruining vines. And in the Gospel of Luke from the New Testament, Jesus refers to Herod Antipas as 'that fox' after he is warned of Herod's plot to kill him, painting the king as a crafty enemy intent on entrapment. The fox's reputation as cunning and deceptive is also equated with false prophets in the Old Testament Book of Ezekiel: 'O Israel, your prophets are like the foxes in the deserts.' In John Gill's *Exposition of the Old Testament*, from the eighteenth century, he explains that these false prophets are 'comparable to foxes, for their craftiness and cunning, and lying in wait to deceive, as these seduced the Lord's people; and such are false teachers, who walk in craftiness, and handle the word of God deceitfully, and are deceitful workers; and to foxes in the deserts, which are hungry and ravenous, and make a prey of whatsoever comes within their reach, as these prophets did of the people.'

These early biblical references to the fox inform the Church's representations of the fox in the Middle Ages, which also tie in with the popular portrayals of the sneaky Reynard character, a familiar image that people would recognise and understand.

There are various examples of the way the fox was depicted in ecclesiastical iconography throughout the

Middle Ages. Firstly, as a simple thief – possibly as a cautionary tale to the local community. In Wells Cathedral, a carving that dates to 1190 shows a fox stealing a goose, inspired by early versions of Renard the Fox and Chanticleer. Sometimes the fox was shown as slinging the goose over its back, a common image in wood carvings across Britain. Although there is anecdotal evidence of people witnessing a fox carrying a goose on its back, this seems extremely unlikely – a fox tends to carry prey in its mouth, often clamped to the head or neck. It is a depiction based on myth rather than observation.

As a myth – as a symbol – the fox had already come to represent the devil in medieval bestiary accounts – those tales with a moral message that usually described animals and their characteristics. 'The fox signifies the Devil in this life,' wrote Philippe de Thaun in the twelfth century. 'To people living carnally he shows pretence of death, till they are entered into evil, caught in his mouth. Then he takes them by a jump and slays and devours them, as the fox does the bird when he has allured it.'

Gradually, the early biblical comparisons of the fox with false prophets also started to become increasingly popular as visual representations, with the fox portrayed as a devil preacher. 'When the fox preaches, beware your geese,' says the proverb. The commonly occurring theme of the fox preaching to geese is partly a satire on false preachers and partly advice to avoid them, with the advent of the Lollards, a rebellious group that appeared in the 1330s, calling for reform of the Church.

In a scene from a French manuscript from the end of the thirteenth century or the first quarter of the fourteenth century, a fox stands on its hind legs, propped up by a bishop's crozier. His long brush trails behind him and his chest is typically whiter, or at least paler, than the rest of his orange body. He wears a bishop's mitre and his tongue is lolling out, which gives the impression he is hungry, predatory, salivating and out of control. He is standing before a group of birds: a falcon, chicken, geese, a stork and a swan, his 'congregation'.

The Stained Glass Museum of Ely Cathedral has a couple of 'devil preacher' scenes in its collection. One, from the late fourteenth century, shows a fox wearing a mitre and dressed up in priest's robes, preaching from a pulpit. The fox has his mouth open with his teeth bared. He looks as if he's smiling and has a slightly psychotic air. The eyebrows are low and deviously angled. He lifts up his clawed hands; one is already clutching a dead goose, his 'fingers' gripping tightly around its neck. He looks out onto a rural scene with a couple of gormless-looking geese, the implication being that they won't be around for much longer. The fox looks frightening, in control and definitely an enemy. The roundel was from Holy Cross in Byfield, discovered in the rectory but probably its original location was in the church.

A similar scene is found on an Ely Cathedral misericord: a fox in a preacher's gown gets close enough to the birds in his congregation to make off with one of them. He is on his hind legs, facing four geese who look enraptured by his sermon. It is a common image in medieval art, found in tapestries, stained glass, drawings, paintings, manuscripts and wood carvings across Europe and in the cathedrals of Bristol, Worcester and Leicester, as well as many parish churches including Ludlow, Beverley and Yorkshire, and at St George's in Windsor. The fox is depicted most often as a bishop but also as a pilgrim, priest, friar, monk or abbot. He always looks sly, crafty and cunning.

The fox remained a beguiling and mysterious animal, a competitor, a predator, a creature little understood and approached with wariness and reluctant admiration. It loomed large in the medieval imagination as a symbol for many of society's ills. Gradually, that started to become expressed through our language.

The first example of the word 'fox' being used to denote artfulness or craftiness is from the late twelfth century, from verse in *The Ormulum* by a monk known as Ormin ('Þatt mann iss fox and hinnderрзæp and full off ille wiless'). By then, 'foxly' was used to mean crafty or cunning. The verb 'to fox', meaning to trick by craft, appeared in 1250, and there was also 'to smell a fox' (to be suspicious) and 'to play the fox' (to act cunningly) – it is possible that the Irish word for 'I play the fox', *sionnachuighim*, is where the word 'shenanigans' comes from. In recognition of its thieving tendencies, there's even the word 'vulpeculated', which specifically means to be robbed by a fox.

There are many other related phrases in English dialect, mostly picking up on the animal's negative connotations in popular tradition: to 'box the fox' means 'to rob an orchard', while a 'fox-sleep' is a 'feigned sleep'. But there are some that are neutral, and even quite charming: 'foxes brewings' means 'a mist which rolls among the trees on the escarpment of the Downs in unsettled weather'.

Around Tudor times, a new connotation arose in the phrases 'to hunt or catch the fox' (to get drunk). There is even a connection between drunkenness and the crafty nature of the fox, based on a prose satire written by Thomas Nashe, an Elizabethan poet and playwright. In his *Pierce Penniless, His supplication to the Divell* (1592), he described the types of drunkenness you might encounter, comparing their characteristics with animals, finishing with the eighth type of drunkard, who is 'fox-drunk when crafty-drunk, as many of the Dutchmen be, that will never bargain but when they are drunk'. The association with drunkenness lasted into the Regency period, with 'to get foxed', but has become a less common phrase in modern times. The fox as 'cunning', however, is now firmly set in our language. 'Cunning as a fox', the 'crafty fox', 'sly as a fox' are metaphors used so often that they have become clichés that appear all over the place. 'Outfoxed' is commonly used to mean getting one up on someone in a crafty way. In a memorable scene from *Blackadder Goes Forth*, Baldrick, typically, has a plan. 'A cunning and subtle one?' drawls Blackadder. 'Yes, sir'. 'As cunning as a fox who's just been appointed professor of cunning at Oxford University?'

As well as craftiness, the fox started to become associated with sexuality – possibly going back to Reynard's rape of the wolf's wife. A pilgrim's badge dating from the fourteenth or fifteenth century shows a fox standing on the back of another fox playing an organ. Another has a fox with an erect penis being led by a chained goose. Experts suggest these might have been a comment on the lust of certain preachers, with the organ representing an actual sexual organ. In other carvings and woodcuts, Brother Reynard stands trial for adultery and rape.

In the early sixteenth century, 'foxy' is found to mean 'foxlike', but it became slang in twentieth-century North America to mean a sexy woman. The first example of that meaning is from 1964 in J. H. Clarke's story *Harlem*. 'Daddy, she was a real fox!' a character says.

The etymology of 'vixen' can be traced back to the Old English word 'fyxen'. The meaning of the vixen as an 'ill-tempered, quarrelsome woman' was first recorded in 1575, according to *Chambers Dictionary of Etymology*. The etymology of the word 'fox' itself can be traced back to Old English, before 830. It is of Germanic origin, and related to the Dutch *vos* and German *Fuchs*. Its exact beginnings are hard to ascertain, but the leading etymologist Anatoly Liberman suggests that the word 'fox' may be related to words meaning 'tail' or 'hairy skin', 'sheen', 'secrecy' or 'offensive smell'.

'Tod' was also a proverbial word for fox, first appearing in the twelfth century in the writings of the Benedictine monk Reginald of Durham. It is found again in the Scottish poem *The Flyting of Dunbar and Kennedie* in 1508. A 'tod's bairns', according to the *Oxford English Dictionary*, means 'an evil brood, or children or persons of bad stock'.

And it's not just in Britain that the fox has entered the language for its questionable qualities; in Finland, for example, if someone has a hidden agenda, they are said 'to have a fox under their arm'. The Finns also have a rather lovely word for the aurora borealis: *revontulet*, which translates as 'foxfire'. The origins are supposedly in a Finnish fable, in which an Arctic fox, running through snow, sprayed up crystals with his tail, causing sparks to fly off into the night sky.

In Tudor times, in Britain, we can still see admiration for the fox's cunning expressed in our language: Shakespeare celebrated it with all but two of thirty-three references to foxes in his plays, paying tribute to their guile. 'If thou were the lion, the fox would beguile thee,' Timon says to Apemantus in *Timon of Athens*. 'No more truth in thee than in a drawn fox,' says Falstaff in *Henry IV Part I* to Mistress Quickly, referring to the trickery played by a fox while it is hunted. In *King Lear*, Edgar refers to the fox as 'sneaky' and 'in stealth'.

It's not just our language in which the fox has clearly left its mark, but also in place names all over Britain: Todmorden, Todwick, Todber and Toddington; Foxcombe Hill, Foxton, Foxearth, Foxholes and Foxfields. In fact, a study conducted by Claire Marriage found that 'fox' was the most popular animal-related place name in England, with 206 named for the fox, 141 for the badger and 37 for the otter. Similarly, taverns and ale houses springing up in the Middle Ages were often named after foxes. There remain 143 pubs called the Fox and Hounds and, among others, the Fox (120), the Fox and Goose (16), the Snooty Fox (10) and more than a handful of pubs called the Fox and Grapes, the Fox and Pheasant, or the Fox and Duck. This may, in part, have been due to the popularity of fox hunting across the country, particularly in the case of names such as the Fox and Hound, but many of these names predate that by some way. Perhaps it's a sign of how widespread the fox was in Britain; perhaps it's an indication of affection for the animal; perhaps it's an indication of the animal's usefulness, having coexisted with us side by side for centuries.

In Ancient Britain, foxes would have been hunted by humans for both their meat and their fur. The fox has never been a popular national dish; it is generally considered inedible. The meat is said to have a strong smell and flavour, and tends to be gamey and dry because there is little fat on the animal. However, in the past it was eaten occasionally, likely due to a lack of any alternative. Predators have rarely featured much in our diet, possibly because of an instinct related to the higher risk of a predator contracting diseases through the consumption of other animals. If the early hunter-gatherers ate fox meat out of desperation, the need to do so would have decreased as soon as farming took off. Soon foxes no longer formed a part of the human diet, and these days their meat is very rarely eaten. There is a recipe for fox casserole from the late celebrity chef Clarissa Dickson Wright that calls for hanging the fox in running water for three days (to combat the dryness of the meat) before stewing it in onion, garlic and tomato for a couple of hours and serving with chestnut pasta. On the whole, though, it is viewed as distasteful, which might explain the repulsed reaction on social media when TV presenter Phillip Schofield ate roadkill fox meat live on air in 2013.

However, an enthusiastic roadkill connoisseur I spoke with protested that fox in lasagne or stir fry, especially if it's the meat of a cub, is delicious.

The fur of the fox would have been much more important, worn to keep warm during harsh winters. Although there is little evidence about fur in ancient times, fox remains turn up in a great deal of archaeological digs from the Anglo-Saxon period onwards. Bones recovered from Saxo-Norman (tenth to twelfth century) deposits recovered at Millbridge, Hertford, were mainly foot and tail bones, which implies that the rest of the body was removed for its pelt, and that the use of fox fur was an established practice. It may have been a popular choice as foxes were relatively numerous and their fur is warm, protective and soft. The individual guard hairs can grow to 5 centimetres, and even longer in colder climates. In a 1986 paper in the *Canadian Journal of Zoology*, Daniel Maurel and a team at the Centre National de la Recherche Scientifique in France compared the hair of the red fox, badger and mink. As well as the guard hairs and fine hairs, they wrote, 'the fox has a third, intermediate, hair type; these correspond to guard hairs but are smaller in size and diameter. In this species, the hairs are grouped in triads: each triad is formed by one guard hair (with its fine hairs) and two intermediate hairs, each having a certain number of fine hairs.' They also found that this affected the overall density of the pelage: 'It is 10 times denser in the fox than in the badger and 10 times denser in the mink than in the fox,' they found, which perhaps suggests why mink has traditionally been a more popular fur than fox.

In the Middle Ages, the fox continued to be useful to humans, possibly still for its meat at this point, but almost certainly for its fur. London became a hive of the fur trade around the thirteenth century, and the 'skinners' – as the fur merchants were called – often had connections with royalty, aristocracy and the Church, which boosted the industry economically. Through the Middle Ages, fur turned from being an essential and practical warming garment to a luxury item, an important signal of hierarchy and upper-class status. Medieval demands for fur were extensive: in one year alone (1344–5), the royal household commissioned 79,220 skins of trimmed miniver (plain white fur used for trimming). Just one of Henry VI's robes required a whopping 12,000 squirrel and 80 ermine skins.

Luckily for the fox, its fur wasn't considered truly luxurious in the early centuries of the fur trade – not compared with ermine, sable or beaver, which were warmer and silkier, and thus more desirable. An essay on the fur trade in the early medieval Mediterranean by James Howard-Johnston suggests that Vikings from the north trading fur with the Caliphate in the ninth and tenth centuries did not value fox pelts highly. He says that the pelts of foxes, along with those of squirrels and tree-martens, were considered 'relatively humdrum', while ermine, sable and miniver were 'prized', as they were more delicate and soft. However, as fur became more of a fashion item, the brilliant hue of fox fur made it increasingly popular, especially for trimmings. The first known mention of 'fox-furred' to mean trimmed with fox fur is from 1501: 'my tawney gown furryd w' ffoxe'. By the beginning of the seventeenth century, fox pelts exported for the European markets were fetching up to 40 shillings each, and the fox-fur trade continued into the twentieth century.

By the Tudor period, the fox had also become an established element of medical practice, its various body parts being used to treat all manner of ailments. This was not a new trend: animal-based remedies had been common for some time, and cures involving parts of the fox had existed since at least the Middle Ages. 'And though he be right guileful in himself and malicious, yet he is good and profitable in use of medicine,' wrote Bartholomaeus Anglicus, a teacher and scholar in the thirteenth century.

We can see a more complete account emerging from Edward Topsell, an Anglican priest, who records the fox's many medical uses in his *History of Four-Footed Beasts* of 1607. (The book also claims that weasels give birth through their ears and lemmings graze in the clouds, but still, it is highly valuable as one of a few historical sources that mention foxes from the time.) The ashes of fox flesh burnt and dunked in wine were said to cure shortness of breath and liver problems. Fox blood was prescribed for bladder stones. Brains fed to infants warded off epilepsy. Fat was used to cure gout and rubbed onto bald heads as a cure for alopecia. Adults were encouraged to tie the penis of a fox around their aching heads to relieve the pain of migraine. Leprosy? Fox poo and vinegar. Blindness? Get a fox's tongue and hang it around your neck. Struggling to breathe? Powder some liver and lungs for assured relief. The testicles were tied around the neck of a child suffering from toothache in what might be considered the least charming necklace in British history.

A useful and admired creature it may have been, but the Tudor period also saw a distinct shift in attitude, and not just towards foxes; in 1532 a death knell sounded for most of Britain's mammals. The Vermin Acts, passed by Henry VIII, introduced statutory legislation with financial reward for killing animals seen as a threat to grain, crops, livestock and eggs. The laws were a response to the struggles of a growing population following the Black Death, the Great Famine, and years of bad harvests caused by excessive rainfall and outbreaks of disease, hunger and poverty. Unwilling to tolerate any competition for resources, the Acts declared that predatory mammals such as foxes, polecats, pine martens and wildcats as well as hedgehogs, rats and birds must be exterminated. In fact, very few animals were exempt: hedgehogs were killed because they were thought to eat eggs and suck the milk from cow's udders; moles for damaging grassland and crops; otters for taking fish; and foxes for preying on piglets, poultry and lambs. It was vital to protect the recovering population from anything that was perceived as a threat, no matter how small it appeared.

The Act decreed that churchwardens painstakingly record the number of different animals killed. They were also in charge of paying out a bounty for the head of each animal. The head of a fox or badger could fetch 12 pence, which was considerably more than the average daily wage of 4 pence. It was a much higher price than for the other wildlife. Before the development of shotguns, foxes were trapped with nets and then beaten to death with sticks or poisoned. The legislation was strengthened by Queen Elizabeth I and would be a profound influence on attitudes towards the control of predatory mammals and carnivores over the ensuing centuries.

People had different attitudes towards the natural world at this time. Animals were seen as expendable objects, creatures that were given to humans by God, and were on the planet only to serve mankind in whatever way human beings saw fit – whether that was food, clothing, labour, sport or entertainment. For example, it was customary to release a fox and a cat in Inner Temple on St Stephen's Day and set the hounds on them as part of the Christmas revelry in the seventeenth century. 'A Huntsman cometh into the Hall, with a fox and a purse-net; with a cat, both bound at the end of a staff; and with them nine or ten couple of hounds, with the blowing of hunting horns. And the fox and cat are by the hounds set upon, and killed beneath the fire. This sport finished, the Marshal placeth them in the several appointed places,' wrote the scholar William Dugdale of the recreational spectators' event, which took place between two courses of food. It is unlikely many in the modern day would be able to eat after witnessing such an episode.

Fox tossing was a much loved pastime for aristocratic couples in seventeenth- and eighteenth-century Europe. The game took place in squares of lawn or courtyard and involved tossing the animal as high as possible from strips of material taut as a tightrope. A good effort was tossing the fox 24 feet high into the air. Usually the animal died, as you'd expect, and large events were sometimes staged involving hundreds of animals: in his book *Hunting Weapons*, Howard Blackmore recounts how 'at a famous contest held at Dresden by the Elector of Saxony, Augustus the Strong (1694–1733), 687 foxes, 533 hares, 34 badgers and 21 wildcats were tossed to their deaths.' Occasionally the sport would take place during a masquerade ball when the players as well as the vulpine participants would be dressed up in masks and costumes.

It was as quarry, however, that animals were increasingly used, as hunting grew ever more popular. For the upper classes, obtaining food was no longer the prime objective – hunting was becoming more about sport and entertainment. And hunting foxes was nothing new: Alexander the Great is one of the earliest known fox hunters; the Romans also engaged in the sport, though with not nearly as much ceremony and import as what would come later; and in the tenth century, King Canute classed foxes as 'Beasts of the Chase' (any animal deemed suitable for hunting). Thanks to the longstanding zeal for hunting of all kinds in Britain, a series of laws was put into place that gradually made the British landscape particularly well suited for hunting. It was the Normans who were the first people so enthusiastic about hunting that they created areas of parkland where game or quarry could be protected. In the eleventh century, William the Conqueror, a keen hunter looking to protect his own interests, set up the Forest Laws, which protected both quarry animals from being killed and their habitats from being destroyed, benefiting wildlife populations and creating an ideal countryside for hunting. The hunting of all animals remained a hobby of the royals, but by the late thirteenth century Edward I had a pack of hounds and a huntsman specifically for foxes, and during the reign of Richard II in the fourteenth century, official public permission was given to hunt the fox.

A significant boon for hunting came about with the Enclosure Acts, from 1604, which converted public land to privately owned land. Large areas, including plenty of ancient woodland, were now fenced off, and a patch-work quilt of green fields bordered by hedgerows began to emerge and spread instead. In terms of hunting, this provided a greater expanse of grassland, which was easier to gallop across, and a network of obstacles, in the form of hedgerows, for jumping, while previously boggy fields were drained, so the ground was dryer and safer to ride rapidly over. The changes had a profound effect on farmers, who had relied on the common land, but also on the deer population, as those lands had formed their habitat.

Foxes were still not the main target of the hunt at this time. In his *Book of Sports*, Pierce Egan wrote that, until the late seventeenth century, 'the fox was considered an inferior animal of the chase, the stag, buck, and even hare, ranking before him'. As the deer population declined, however, hunters turned their attention to other quarry. The fox was really the only mammal left that was worth hunting, now that the main motive was recreation and sport. It was Britain's last remaining large native mammal, alongside the badger: the wolves (last seen in 1680), bears (1000) and beavers (1526) had all vanished as a result of intensive hunting and habitat decline. Smaller mammals such as the pine marten, polecat and wild cat had also mostly disappeared,

either driven to near-extinction for their fur or exterminated to protect game birds. And so fox hunting started to
take off.

In the mid-eighteenth century, the Vermin Acts were finally
repealed. By that time, Britain was a much easier place to
live in than in medieval and Tudor times: the country was
relatively prosperous, more politically and socially stable,
and healthcare was much improved. Because there was
more food to go round, people were not in competition
with foxes in the same way they had been, so there wasn't
as much of a need to protect grain, crops or people by
slaughtering hedgehogs and other animals. It is impossible
to quantify how successful the Acts had been in keeping
human populations alive and fed, but certainly Britain's
wildlife populations paid a heavy and irreversible price,
with many disappearing completely. Fox populations were
hit hard: records before hunting took off are scarce, but we
know numbers were wiped out in some areas by the Vermin
Laws, and didn't recover for many years. In surviving parish
accounts of the animals killed, it is the fox that appears most
consistently – between six and twelve foxes a year in English
parishes considered places of 'high control'.

Fox control certainly didn't stop overnight. The animal
was still considered vermin by farmers and the shooting

community. The last record of a fox killed and recorded by a parish was in Bedfordshire in 1820. However, that too was about to change as it started to become the favourite quarry of a countryside sport that was rapidly growing in popularity.

The catalyst that had caused fox hunting to lurch into a national sport was a change in the way it was organised in the 1750s. Aristocrats introduced rules, regulations, funding and, crucially, the breeding of faster hounds and horses. It took a few committed leaders to catapult fox hunting into the mainstream. Hugo Meynell, described by fellow hunter Dick Christian as a 'regular little apple dumpling on horseback', was one of them; he was the Master of the Quorn hunt in Leicestershire, the county with the most legendary 'hunting country'. Known as the 'father of fox hunting', he bred foxhounds and thoroughbred horses for greater speed and stamina. The hunt soon became fast and exciting, with a new element of high-octane riding. Men in smart red coats and top hats would gallop freely on the finest horses across the most exquisite stretches of British countryside, unfettered by roads or railways, pursuing foxhounds with beautifully dappled coats in cream, brown and black and vertical tails. It was a raucous scene: the yearning note of the hunting horn, the cries of the hounds and the developing language of the hunting men. Most people would never see a hunt, as they took place on private land, but for anyone who did, it would pass in a flash, such was the speed of the chase. A common spectacle was the hunt meet, which might take place at a public landmark. It was moved from dawn to the much more reasonable hour of II a.m., giving time to hobnob and socialise together. This also meant that people could travel from other regions of the country to take part.

The 'golden age' of fox hunting (roughly from 1800 to 1870) was in full swing. It was a time when the countryside was still relatively unspoilt by barbed wire and motorways, and the hunt had a greater freedom of movement. The sport had evolved into something fast, furious and exciting for its proponents, and took place on a regular basis all around the country – the aristocracy often had six days a week free to dedicate to the sport. And there were fewer opponents and conflicting interests to interfere with their activities, whether in the shape of animal rights advocates, farmers or gamekeepers.

As hunting took off, the fox's position was elevated in country circles. He became a shining example of a worthy foe, not just vermin to be killed without ceremony, and the focus was very much back on his intelligence and cunning. As this view became more widespread, the fox depicted in books and pictures started to change. Instead of being part of a long European tradition of the fox as trickster, devil preacher or chicken-pincher, the fox was now the top quarry, illustrated in the hunting literature as 'Charlie'.

Just as hunting changed the way foxes were treated and perceived in Britain by enhancing their recreational value, so, too, did it influence the way they were written about. No longer solely depicted as the villain, they were increasingly portrayed as an admirable creature and a worthy foe. As the painter J. C. Dollman of *The Fox O' One Tree Hill* put it, 'an the beautiful creetur, worth pounds an pounds, A specially made to be killed by hounds'.

There is an argument, in fact, that the popularity of fox hunting is responsible for keeping the fox alive as a species in Britain. As we've seen, the Vermin Acts, other population controls and the fur trade had all taken a terrible toll on fox populations. Foxes sometimes had to be caught and released in the right place for hunting, which suggests numbers were dwindling, although this practice was scorned by certain hunt circles who felt hunting a 'bagged' fox was bad sport. But as the fox was now seen as something useful – a noble quarry – there was a push to boost numbers, even importing them from Europe. Imported foxes were sold for 10 shillings at Leadenhall market in 1845, and DNA analysis suggests that foxes in the South of England are much more closely related to French foxes than those from the North of England. Cubs were also preserved and coverts managed to encourage the fox population. So it is possible that without the need to protect the fox for man's pleasure and as a sporting incentive, it would have gone the same way as the wolf, bear and lynx. That argument existed as early as Tudor times: 'If foxes were not preserved for the pleasure of gentlmen they would be utterly destroyed manie years agone,' wrote chronicler Raphael Holinshead to Elizabeth I.

It would be somewhat ironic if the survival of the species was largely thanks to the desire to hunt it. But arguably, although the population was probably enhanced by hunting, the fox might have survived in any case, owing to its relative size, making it far less of a threat to humans than, for example, the wolf, and its resilience and adaptability as a species.

Hunting not only had an effect on fox populations; it also became a key architect of the British countryside landscape alongside agriculture. Spinneys were encouraged and gorse coverts were planted to provide habitats that would be easy to drive foxes out of, as opposed to large woods – between 1800 and 1850 the amount of gorse in Leicestershire is said to have doubled in an effort to give foxes habitat. Many of these areas still stand, and it is possible that the modern British landscape would have even less woodland than it does today without hunting.

The popularity of fox hunting also created tension between proponents of the sport and farmers, who still saw the fox as a pest. By the late 1800s, it was frowned on to shoot foxes. Sporting magazines would even publish the names of known fox-murderers. The split between those who saw the fox as something that needed to be conserved so that it could be hunted and those who wanted to exterminate it in order to protect their livestock or game became even more pronounced through the nineteenth century as farming intensified. More land was taken up by agriculture and the hunt had to persuade the farmers, who loathed foxes and wanted them dead, to keep them alive. It is a paradoxical conundrum and a sometimes strained pact that exists to this day.

Pheasant shooting began in the same period, which added another human interest: the development of the shooting estate. The gamekeepers who looked after the land and the shoot didn't want foxes around to take their birds. In an issue of *Sporting Review* magazine published in 1869, the clash between fox hunting and shooting is explored and a sportsman called Captain Percy Williams is quoted as saying, 'Pheasants have brought in their train envy, hatred and malice, have dispossessed the fox and demoralised the country.' All these conflicting interests meant that emotions were running high.

The hunt and the tensions it inspires are unique to Britain. British huntsmen did introduce their practice of hunting on horseback around the world, and hunting groups sprang up in North America, Ireland, Italy, France, Canada and Australia (the red fox was introduced there in 1833 for the sole purpose of hunting). But hunting in other countries never quite took off as it had in the UK, in terms of the number of hunts and packs per area, for various reasons. In France, for example, farmers were not amenable to allowing their land to be used for sport. 'The farmers have no idea of people riding over their land, or what they call "chase à cheval",' wrote Colonel John Cook in his book *Observations on Fox-Hunting*, published in 1826, adding that the country would be 'up in arms' if one attempted partridge shooting. The French people he knew didn't believe you could train a hound to kill only foxes.

Hunting was popular in the United States, but really it was a different sport altogether. The focus was – and is – on the chase, not the kill. The fox doesn't face death at all, and it is often called 'fox chasing'. 'A successful hunt ends when the fox is accounted for by entering a hole in the ground, called an earth. Once there, hounds are rewarded with praise from their huntsman. The fox gets away and is chased another day,' says the Masters of Foxhounds Association of America's website. Often the hunt chases coyotes or bobcats instead of foxes.

There have been hunts across Europe, but not to the same extent as in Britain, where there were scores of hunts in every area of the country. Currently there are 186 packs of foxhounds in England, Wales and Scotland and 41 in Ireland. Elsewhere the numbers are lower: France and Italy (3 each), Portugal (1) and Australia (19). In Britain the hunt became part of the countryside economy and cultural fabric, embedded in rural identity.

The landscape played a key part in hunting's popularity, but there were other factors. Perhaps it was a result of horse breeding in Britain that led to hunts taking place at breakneck speed. After the near-invasion by the Spanish Armada in 1588, Elizabeth I was determined to improve her cavalry, particularly focusing on the quality and speed of the horses themselves. Three Eastern stallions – the Darley Arabian, the Godolphin Barb and the Byerley Turk – were imported, and, soon, the great English thoroughbred was reared, 'the supreme horse of the world in speed, courage and quality', according to Wilson Stephens' essay 'How We Inherited Hunting'. These magnificent new breeds meant that fox hunting could evolve from a slow, standard plod to a high-speed national obsession. The thrill element was born.

Hound breeding also took place specifically in Britain, and greatly improved as the eighteenth century drew on. This pattern of evolution might have carried over even to the fox and fox hunters, wrote Stephens, suggesting that 'foxes that could not run and think fast enough to outwit the ever quicker foxhounds did not live to hand on their failings to another generation' and that the hunting man had to evolve 'to sustain conditions in which they could remain happy in their sport'.

The manners and etiquette of early hunting chimed perfectly with Victorian society and the idea of the 'manly' 'gentleman' and ideals of courage and courtesy. 'The hunting field acquired what it had previously lacked, that element of daredevilry and decision which the Elizabethan sailors had shown in the war against Spain, which the men of Marlborough and Wellington were soon to show, which came out again generations later in the Battle of Britain, and which will always come out in time of challenge so long as Britons remain Britons,' wrote Stephens.

Perhaps fox hunting remained and prospered because it supported a prevailing idea of British identity: that of the gallant but dominating survivor.

The 'Golden Age of Hunting' waned as farming and industry spread through the nineteenth century, reducing expanses of open country and limiting how far the hunts could ride. Canals, railways and, later, an increase in roads and motorways also truncated hunting country. Hunters at the time thought the Industrial Revolution would be the death of hunting, but it did manage to evolve. It took another hit when life in Europe was ruptured by the First World War and many British huntsmen left to serve and did not return. However, those who made it back were eager to take part again. Stephens writes that the 1920s 'saw a regeneration in all aspects of the sport', because young men who had had war-time adventures returned keen to broaden their horizons. There were fears that the Second World War would rupture the hunting world, but again, according to Stephens, the link between the 'fearlessness' of the hunting code and the necessary fearlessness of war kept the sport alive in the minds of those at home and away. The fighter pilots in the Battle of Britain called out 'Tally Ho!' – the sound a huntsman makes when he see a fox – as they faced the Germans. When the war ended, hunting in Britain was maintained by new and old fans.

Of course, not everyone was pleased that hunting endured. The animal welfare movement had showed signs of starting as early as 1740, when protesting voices began to be heard regarding hunting in general, including such high-profile figures as Jeremy Bentham speaking out for animals: 'The question is not, Can they *reason*? Nor, Can they *talk*? but Can they *suffer*?' And it had finally become a political issue in 1800 when the first Bill – against bear baiting – was submitted. The animal rights movement and anti-hunting groups were gathering strength, fuelled by respected and influential voices such as Bentham, John Stuart Mill and Henry Salt, central figures in many of the intellectual debates of their day. They agitated, wrote, published and posed questions to the public and members of parliament that no one had done before. In 1824, the Society for the Prevention of Cruelty to

Animals was formed (later, the RSPCA – it was given royal support through patronage in 1840 from Queen Victoria) and soon after, bear baiting (1825), badger baiting (1835) and cock fighting (1849) were banned.

So far, the fox hunt had not been affected, but in 1869, a controversial essay, written by the historian E. A. Freeman, looked at the fox in a new way, questioning the morality of fox hunting specifically for the first time. Freeman didn't hold back in his attack on the 'savage' sport, calling it cowardly and foolhardy. The novelist Anthony Trollope replied to Freeman that hunting was a bearer of 'national efficiency', making Englishmen 'what they are' and keeping them that way. He denounced Freeman as a milksop and bookworm and argued that there was no comparison between fox hunting and bear baiting: very few huntsmen watch the actual death of the fox, which for him was inconsequential. A storm of opinion, emotion and response erupted, played out in the pages of the *Daily Telegraph* and the *Guardian*, much as it does today. The spotlight had finally settled on the issue of fox hunting, and it began to be discussed seriously for the first time.

By no means did any of this happen overnight: the treatment of animals continued during the nineteenth century much as it always had. There is a carpet of green lawn called Weston's Yard in the middle of Eton College, where I used to play as a child with other teachers' families. I remember a game where we'd roll each other up in rugs like sausage rolls amid gleeful hysterics. A very different type of sport took place in the buildings nearby during the nineteenth century. The college butcher provided a ram that would be hunted and beaten to death by the pupils. Then, on Shrove Tuesday, the college cook would pin a crow to a pancake and hang it on a door to serve as a target. 'Even in the nineteenth century such sports as bull-baiting, badger-baits, dog fights, and cat and duck hunts were organised for the special edification of the Eton boys,' wrote Henry Salt, a master at the school in the 1890s.

Salt was a compelling advocate for animal rights and welfare. It is interesting that such an unconventional, counter-cultural mind could arise from one of the most traditional institutions in the country (he studied there before returning to teach). Eton's history of blood sports disgusted Salt. He believed the services of hunting were no longer required and that blood sports were an anachronism, a 'relic of savagery', which time would gradually remove. He campaigned against the Royal Buckhounds – a stag-hunt pack – and the Eton Beagles, and was, in effect, the first saboteur, although the methods he used were very different from those employed today, consisting mainly of writing treatises and petitioning the headmaster. The published accounts of spectators at the time are forerunners to the updates written on the Facebook walls and forums of the Hunt Saboteurs Association and the HSA magazine *Howl* in the present day. They read similarly: highly detailed and exact, with an undercurrent of revulsion. On a hare hunt near Upton Park and Slough Road, a witness wrote in 1899, 'Its condition of terror and exhaustion was painful to behold.' Then follows graphic descriptions of the hare being dismembered, her feet handed around for trophies, before her stomach was split open and the corpse thrown to the hounds. It was called the 'breaking up' of the hare.

Salt's decade-long campaign against the Royal Buckhounds was successful, but it would take longer for hare hunts to stop at Eton. At the same time as Salt's work and writings were published, the Protection of Animals Act in 1911 was passed, to protect domestic and captive wild animals from harm and abuse.

Concurrently, children's literature began to evolve into stories with a newly compassionate purpose, containing lessons about cruelty, kindness, conservation, natural history and social morality. No longer were stories about animals simply a metaphor for human behaviour; people were interested in the animals themselves, not just as objects to be used in whatever manner humans saw fit, but as individual creatures. By the nineteenth century animal autobiographies such as *Black Beauty* (1877, about a horse) and *Beautiful Joe* (1893, about a dog) had become highly popular.

Foxes as central characters, though, were scarce. They

crop up in Beatrix Potter, although there's certainly still a whiff of Reynard in her characters – when reaching for a villain, she often cast a fox. In *The Tale of Jemima Puddle-Duck*, a revision of 'Little Red Riding Hood', the fox is suave, civil and handsome. He is reading the newspaper when we first meet him. He lures his new friend Jemima to his house, and she enters, although she's a little surprised at the amount of feathers. He offers her a safe and dry place to lay her eggs and suggests a dinner party, for a treat. We are told that Jemima is a simpleton, that she doesn't realise that he plans to kill and eat her. She tells Kep, a collie on the farm, about the plan and he arrives with a couple of foxhounds. The foxy-whiskered gentleman is no more.

The Tale of Mr Tod was one of Potter's later books and it arose from a fatigue she felt in writing 'goody goody books about nice people'. Instead, she wanted to write about two disagreeable people, called Tommy Brock and Mr Tod, one a badger, the other a fox. Tommy is actually the worse scoundrel of the two, stealing rabbit babies from old Mr Bouncer. The fox isn't cunning or wily in the same way as Reynard, and Potter portrays him almost sympathetically (even though his house is a filthy cave filled with horrible things like rabbit skulls). Reynard may lurk in Potter's representation, but he is less of a terrifying carnivore.

The great French children's book by Antoine de Saint-Exupéry, *The Little Prince* (1943), provides one of the first occasions on which a fox emerges as a good character in its own right. It gives wisdom and knowledge to the little alien boy who's fallen to earth from a tiny asteroid. The fox also says this: 'Men. They have guns, and they hunt. It is very disturbing. They also raise chickens. These are their only interests.' It is striking that the fox was the creature chosen to preach a moral message and to teach the boy the book's crucial lessons about human existence, friendship, loneliness and contentment – certainly a change from the traditional Reynard character.

In the latter part of the twentieth century, drawing on the work of thinkers such as Henry Salt, animal rights movements gained momentum with the formation of various organisations, from the Oxford Group, a cabal of intellectuals who furthered the concept of animal rights, to the Hunt Saboteurs Association, PETA and multiple animal rescue centres. Their first victory was over the fur trade, which had had a major resurgence in the nineteenth and twentieth centuries. Fox fur as a fashion item reached the height of its popularity in the 1930s, when fur stoles and collars were popular with women. Fox stoles complete with the head and paws were often worn in Hollywood films. Marilyn Monroe was a fan of the fur, as were Lana Turner and Grace Kelly.

Fur farms had sprung up to support the trade, breeding animals specifically for their pelts. Such farms were based mainly in other European countries and in Canada – there are records of hunting for fur and fur farms in Britain, too, but most concerned mink rather than fox. The *Daily Mail* did report, in April 1923, a proposal for a ranch of fur-bearing animals, including blue and white foxes, and skunks. The Arctic fox was much more popular with trappers in Alaska, who culled populations of red fox to keep the more expensive Arctic fox thriving. Another report in the *Daily Mail*, from July 1921, offers a breakdown of the animals bred in captivity on Canada's fur farms. Out of 8,000 fur-bearing animals, 7,000 were silver black foxes, 850 were patch foxes and nearly 300 were red foxes.

In 2000, farming wild animals for fur was banned in Britain. As public opinion about fur has soured, genuine farmed fox pelts are now often sold as fake fur. Compared with other animals, *Vulpes vulpes* has survived its trade as an item of clothing – many animals haven't.

But where the animal rights debate has raged most fiercely around foxes is with regard to hunting. The twentieth century was a time of a rancorous split in the feeling towards both fox hunting and foxes, fuelled by the modern animal rights movement, which led to hunt sabotage and animal activism. The fox in modern times is a story of fierce emotional warfare, conservation politics and animal rights. It is a bitterly fought war. Often those supporting a hunting ban or animal rights are criticised by association. The

Countryside Alliance, for example, compared Tony Blair with Hitler during the furore over the hunting ban in the early years of the present century: 'Hitler banned fox hunting partly because he wanted to attack the aristocracy's way of life and further his own ambitions. It would appear that Tony Blair's reasons for banning fox hunting are not dissimilar – a curious mixture of class envy, spite and a curious understanding of animal welfare,' said a spokesperson for the Countryside Alliance.

While opinion is still firmly divided on that subject, the way foxes are portrayed and perceived in popular culture has certainly undergone a change. In *Mary Poppins* (1964), Bert, Mary and the children jump into one of Bert's chalk drawings of the countryside and find themselves in a kind of benign acid trip featuring dancing penguins, escaped carousel horses and a fox hunt. The hunters are characterised as snooty and posh, their noses upturned in disapproval beneath their top hats, and their horses all silly and ignoble. The Cockney one-man-band Bert spots the fox – 'Poor little bloke, let's give him a hand' – and sweeps in, tooting an imaginary horn and scooping up the humorous canid. Bert was essentially a hunt saboteur, using one of the strategies (blowing a hunting horn) to disrupt the hunt that is still used to this day. Disney, it seems, was firmly pro-fox: the unequivocal hero in Disney's *Robin Hood* (1973) is played by a fox, as is Maid Marian, the prettiest vixen on film, while

The Fox and the Hound (1981) is about the unlikely friendship between two would-be adversaries.

No longer is Reynard the archetypal fox – occasionally he might crop up in a children's story or a fox might be referred to as 'Reynard' in the letters pages of traditional British newspapers; but it is no longer the go-to fox in British culture – that distinction now belongs to Fantastic Mr Fox, the first of many friendly fox heroes.

These days our environment is so depleted that seeing a fox is a lucky thrill for many and most people are more likely to seek out nature than want to destroy it. A significant part of the population is interested in animals and nature, seen clearly in the enduring popularity of David Attenborough documentaries and the BBC's 'Watches' franchise (*Springwatch*, *Autumnwatch* and *Winterwatch*).

From high-street shops selling Lush and Body Shop products through the 1980s and 1990s to clothes and accessory shops stocking tea towels, necklaces and jumpers emblazoned with foxes, the fox is an increasingly popular symbol. The people of Britain are known for their relationship with and fondness for animals and pets. The RSPCA was, after all, the world's first animal welfare charity. It is not surprising then that, as consumerism grew in post-war Britain, the number of shops selling animal-themed items would increase. The fox has become a bit of a cult icon in establishments such as Oliver Bonas and Joy; perhaps that's partly a result of the pro-fox movement, and sympathy for a perceived victim; perhaps it's simply because people find it a striking and beautiful creature. Whatever the reason, it seems that the traditional cultural depictions of the fox as villain or vermin are increasingly behind us.

Nowadays, we would be surprised to see the publication of a children's book in the Reynard form. Instead, *The Fox and the Star* by Coralie Bickford-Smith is about a fox who lives in a deep, dark forest and has only one friend, Star. One night Star disappears, and Fox has to face the forest alone. It is a tale of grief and coming to terms with loss and was named Waterstones Book of the Year in 2015. *Pax*, by Sara Pennypacker, tells the story of a boy and his pet fox. His father enters military service and the boy has to return the fox to the wild. The fox in these popular modern tales is a benign force, a friend, a support; it could not be more different from the lip-smacking Mr Tod or even Fantastic Mr Fox. The fox is a creature worthy of our love – and capable of reciprocating it.

The fox has always been a topic of controversy, dividing opinion between those who admire its wily nature and those who revile it for its carnivorous tendencies. The story became increasingly complicated as the popularity of hunting took off, creating very distinct rural and class identities, and adding an extra dimension to the divide in opinion. All of this has combined to make modern British attitudes towards the fox unique. Despite the fact that the fox now has a more positive image in our culture, it is still a highly controversial creature, often heavily vilified in the media, and the hunting dispute rages as fiercely as ever.

But despite all the many strongly held opinions and ferociously argued debates, ultimately not that much is widely known about the fox itself. A great deal of our ideas, perceptions and attitudes are based on myth, folklore, hearsay and literature, which over the years have frequently been distorted and exaggerated, and often accepted as truth. Many of our ideas, then, are a complete fiction. By looking at some of the fox's habits and behaviours, perhaps we can reclaim some of the facts.

2

Fox in the Henhouse

The fox is a skilled hunter, an impressive product of evolution and adaptation. It's one of the things that makes attitudes towards the animal profoundly problematic in a human-dominated environment – and lies at the root of much of the dislike and demonisation the fox inspires. But does it deserve its reputation?

Foxes are not fussy eaters. They are omnivores, happy to feed on a variety of plants and animals, remarkably successful at adapting to different environments, from desert to glacial to urban landscapes. If its environment changes, as a result of climate change, for example, the fox will respond, adapting its habits and diet to hunt and survive in new conditions. As higher latitudes warm up, foxes will move north – as a recent story from Canada illustrates.

Don Gutoski headed out into Wapusk National Park to photograph polar bears before they made their way to Hudson Bay to hunt seals. Nature had always helped him relax and de-stress from his job as an A&E doctor; the land on which he lives he leaves uncultivated, free to grow wild. On this particular day, it was −30°C outside and Gutoski wasn't sure what he'd find.

Suddenly, he spotted a red fox, an animal not often found that far north in the Canadian tundra, and certainly one he was not expecting to see. The fox was chasing something. It looked like a flare of rust against the snowy plain, its body elongated as its legs galloped and stretched. As Gutoski got closer he could see that it had already caught its prey in its mouth. It was an Arctic fox. He realised he was seeing something highly unusual. He set up his camera and spent a total of three hours waiting to get the perfect shot. 'I was very surprised not only to see two predators fight, but also the victor eating its prey, which is unusual in the natural world,' he said.

Gutoski entitled the best photograph of the series he took that day 'A Tale of Two Foxes' and submitted it for the Natural History Museum's Wildlife Photographer of the Year prize in 2015; it won. The image is arresting. Against a backdrop of grey snow, a bright orange fox with a ruffled white chest and its tail, ending in a furry white bob, curled round, half squats. Its head is bowed down, and its eyes squeezed tightly shut. In its mouth is the dead and bloody carcass of the smaller Arctic fox, also with its head down and eyes shut, its body dangling like a white towel.

That is not a sight we are likely to see in Britain, but our red fox is also constantly adapting its diet in order to get the 600 or so calories a day it needs, depending on the time of year and the location of its territory.

In spring, earthworms are one of its favoured foods, surfacing on mild, calm nights, often just after it has rained. Once found, they're pulled out of the ground like a strand of spaghetti and gobbled up, or saved for the cubs. A single fox can eat hundreds in one night. Birds also form part of the spring diet, as do the afterbirth of lambs and stillborn lambs. Foxes can nip up trees quite nimbly and snatch young birds from nests – and if the nests are on the ground, it's even easier.

Foxes love berries, which start appearing in May; if they're lucky they will happen upon gooseberries, rising on their hind legs to pluck fruit off the bush, and sugary strawberries, growing on the ground, an easier fruit to snaffle. Crane flies hatching in June bring a bonanza for the fox, who can eat hundreds at a time. Foxes will also hoover up crane-fly larvae –'leatherjackets'. In the high summer, they eat crunchy, protein-rich grasshoppers and beetles, and as summer turns to autumn feast on plums, apples, blackberries, bilberries and other fruits.

Crane flies are also in abundance across the country by autumn, emerging at night to chew on plant stems, providing a perfect opportunity for the nocturnal fox. In winter, foxes rely mainly on smaller mammals such as mice and rabbits, and perhaps any insects that are still braving the colder weather.

The geography and ecology of a fox's territory also

heavily influence its diet. In some areas of the countryside, voles will be the main source of energy, in others it might be carrion or worms. Near the sea, a fox may also feed on the carrion it finds there (birds and even seals) or on crabs; in forest areas, woodland mammals; and in river and lake areas, frogs.

Town foxes still eat wild food – those in Central London will eat more pigeons and rats than the fox populations living in the suburbs – but of course they will also scavenge and forage food littered by humans or deliberately left out for them. Foxes will eat most processed foods, such as fried chicken, biscuits, burgers and porridge. One person I spoke to said foxes particularly love marmite sandwiches, while in a cemetery in London, bagels left out on gravestones were quickly swiped, possibly by the local foxes (though the cemetery is teeming with wildlife; perhaps it was a local murder of crows.

The amount a fox scavenges varies from town to town: a study published in Stephen Harris and Phil Baker's *Urban Foxes* (2001) comparing foxes in Bristol and London found that foxes scavenged around 64 per cent of their diet in Bristol and only 35 per cent in the capital. Mostly, the 'human' food foxes eat will have been left out by a fox-lover. Although foxes have a reputation for rifling through bins, they are not usually big or heavy enough to tip over a normal-sized city dustbin, although they might manage to dislodge a bin lid. It is true that if a plastic bag filled with food waste is left out on a street, any roaming animal – whether fox, dog or cat – might rip it open, but that can be avoided by not leaving bags out overnight or by putting them in a proper bin. If you spot a fox trotting down the pavement after dark, it's likely to be sniffing and snooping around for some easy supper.

Much of what I'd learned about fox behaviour and habits was from literature and academic journals, so I wanted to find out what they were like in the flesh. Wildlife photographer Richard Bowler was posting photos of foxes on Twitter. One photo that caught my attention was of a young-looking vixen sitting on his sofa. In the corner of the room was a barn owl. The BBC programme *Springwatch* was on the television. With a bit of digging, I discovered that Richard had a few foxes living on his land. His photos were stunning and he had quite a following on the internet, each image posted receiving lots of online engagement – re-posts, likes and comments. We started a correspondence via email and I asked if I could come over and spend some time with his foxes in North Wales. I discovered that it's not actually that rare to keep foxes as pets, but people tend to keep quiet about it. Richard was adamant that his foxes were not pets; he cared for them rather than kept them. Fen and Rosie lived outside in a huge run; Hetty, just eight weeks old, lived indoors.

I took a bus through Denbighshire, heady at the height of spring, through Llangollen and over the River Dee, its aqueduct-style bridge on my left and the Berwyn mountains providing the backdrop. Richard picked me up from the bus stop and we drove to where he lived with his partner, Helen, on a hill that they'd bought and turned into a wildlife idyll, after searching for a quieter, rural life a few years before. He wore khaki-coloured clothes – the uniform of a nature photographer – glasses and an earring. We arrived, and the couple welcomed me to their home. I couldn't wait to see a fox up close and – bonus – there was the barn owl, perched imperiously on the bookshelf above us, drifting in and out of sleep.

The fox smell hit me as I walked into the living room. It was a strange, musky, aromatic, deep stink that suggested we were in the presence of something wild.

That very distinctive fox smell is usually urine. It is thought that the musky smell is caused by the compound isopentyl methyl sulfide. The reason why the odour is so intense is because foxes use scent regularly as an important marker in the way they interact with each other. It might be used to remind a fox that a cache site is empty, for example, and that it shouldn't bother digging; it might be a sign of being ready to mate.

The zoologist David Macdonald has studied foxes at close quarters for many years. When his fox Niff was on heat she would make more urine marks, as many as a hundred on just one walk, and the smell had a higher pungency. Scent marks may also be a way of communicating within groups, indicating either hierarchy or simply presence.

Foxes are territorial animals, and urine is often used to mark the extent of the territory and to communicate to other foxes that a particular area is taken. The size of territory can vary considerably. One of the factors determining how big a fox group's home turf will be is the availability of food. They will weigh up how much they need against the cost of defending an area against intruders. Food supply also dictates the number of animals living in the territory. Sometimes foxes live in pairs, but often they live in groups, depending on the availability of resources and mortality rates.

In rural areas, such as deep in the safety of the forest, where food isn't scarce, there is often a bit of flexibility over turf, but in urban areas, where successful scavenging forms a larger part of a fox's diet, the borders are normally respected with utmost precision. Macdonald tracked a vixen called Toothypeg and her group members and found that even though they went near a caravan site that offered tasty scraps, they didn't trespass into it at all. Neighbouring groups can be very hostile and aggressive in response to any transgressions.

Males, in particular, can travel incredible distances to find a new territory. In 2014, a fox named Fleet, tracked by a team for the BBC series *Winterwatch*, travelled about 315 kilometres in the space of a month around East Sussex – the equivalent of taking a trip up to Manchester from London. A fox has been recorded travelling in a straight line a distance of 500 kilometres in Sweden; another journeyed 394 kilometres in the United States. The average fox will travel the breadth of four to six territories, a distance of between 15 and 35 kilometres, to find a territory of its own. Often it will have to cross busy roads or even swim across rivers. Male foxes spend winter looking for a new territory and a mate, so such distances might also avoid the risks of inbreeding within their own social group.

So a fox's urine is a very important scent marker, and perhaps that is one of the reasons why it is so pungent. But there are also other smells associated with foxes. One of the other sources for the very acrid aroma, I would discover from the naturalist and broadcaster Chris Packham during one of the more unusual Saturday morning conversations I've ever had, is secreted from their anal glands. The sacs contain a bitter-smelling milky fluid, a rich mixture of fermented bacteria, sweat and dry skin. The violet gland is found near the base of the tail, and is so called because the scent it produces is reminiscent of the flower, though a little unpleasant. Foxes waft the smell around with their tail towards other foxes' faces. We're not sure why; perhaps it is an act of aggression. There are also smell-producing glands in the skin between the toes and the foot pads, and it is this scent that the hounds pick up during a hunt.

Whichever of these sources it may be from, the over-powering smell was not something I got used to during my encounters with foxes, though people who work with foxes adapt to it – and some even profess to like it. Certainly this first experience of it was intense, but I was keen to discover more about Richard's interest in the fox – and to see the animals up close.

Ten years ago, Richard, a keen angler and photographer, wasn't particularly interested in foxes or opposed to hunting. Everything changed when he photographed his first fox and started to become obsessed by their characters. Each fox, he said, has its own personality, and he is completely fascinated by them. 'The first time you get a fox in your lens, there is just something about it,' he said. 'It's the ultimate species to photograph. They're just so good-looking. They've got so much character. When you get to know foxes, it's almost as if you can read their moods. They almost talk to you with their vocalisations.'

Richard's photographs of foxes have sold all over the world. As his career grew, benefiting from his live-in companions, so did his knowledge of the true nature of the animal. 'They're not out to get anyone. They're looking after number one, but they're *really* good at looking after number one,' he said. 'If you spend time with foxes you realise how intelligent they are.'

He certainly sees that intelligence in Hetty. If he puts down a toy and a treat for Maddy, his dog, the fox spots it straight away, but won't go for it immediately. She pauses and walks around the room – 'I'm not interested, I'm not interested' – and waits until the coast is clear before swiping the toy away.

Richard tried to tempt Hetty out of her cage with a piece of beef jerky, but my presence made her unwilling. Foxes are strangely shy and private when they eat. Often they'll turn their backs away from other foxes while they nibble their prey. If one fox approaches another while it's eating, it would expect an aggressive bark or a yap. It is a cardinal sin.

Eventually Hetty allowed Richard to carry her out and I was so close I could touch her. She was beautiful, with pale, almost yellowish fur and a white patch on her throat and neck, creeping up to her face. She was slim, with big pointy ears tipped with black; light brown, amber-coloured eyes, and a moist nose, black as rubber. Her legs and brush were tinged with darker fur. She seemed cautious but strangely confident and alert too. She was like a sweet, feminine, pretty little dog. I felt that she looked clever but wondered if that impression was down to my years of cultural conditioning. It was a strange feeling to be near to something so wild, mercurial and normally untouchable. I realised how layered my own perceptions of foxes were at that moment, cluttered by opinions, rumours and myths. I wanted to hold her but she also commanded a strange kind of respect; it didn't feel right to stroke her or touch her.

Foxes, Richard explained to me, are a bit like cats: they want you on their own terms. 'When Rosie wants to be fussed, she'll run up, ears down, tail wagging. You can't ignore her, you've got to go over there and give her a fuss. Other times I go in there and think, "I'll give her a fuss", and she doesn't want to know.'

I wanted to observe the foxes' body language, but they were shy the day I visited. By the time Hetty had relaxed, her ears had pricked, which suggested she was in a playful mood. When foxes are aggressive or fearful, they'll adopt postures such as an arched body with a lashing tail and ears pulled back, to appear dominant or threatening, while a submissive fox will have legs crouched, ears flattened backwards and its back again arched. Hetty seemed rather shy and timid, with eyes widened, taking in everything in her surroundings.

Richard and Helen had reared Hetty from one week old. She'd been captive-bred and suffered a bad cut on her front leg. The couple was asked to look after her and said yes. They bathed, massaged and hand-reared her through the nights at the beginning. She was so young that she was still deaf and blind when she arrived, so she quickly bonded with Richard and Helen and their terrier Maddy. Indeed, one of Richard's most popular photos on social media was of Hetty and Maddy playing together, posted to make a point that it wasn't natural for hounds to attack foxes, or for dogs and foxes to fight.

I wondered if Richard had got any criticism or backlash from anti-fox types. Plenty, it turned out. Comments on social media such as 'the only good fox is a dead fox' or 'I'd like to see a picture of her with a pack of hounds chasing her' had once bothered him, but these days he's learned to block people who post negatively. What does concern him is the possibility of the local hunt coming through and taking his foxes. And he has reason to be concerned: in the sheep-rearing areas of Wales, there is a fear of foxes taking lambs, and many people see the fox as nothing more than a bloodthirsty hunter, preying on their livestock.

Foxes are very capable of finding all sorts of prey. One of the secrets of their success is agility. A fox can jump, squeeze, run, twist, turn and balance exceptionally well thanks to its long tail. Its legs are also relatively long compared with the length of its spine, which endows it with swift movement and great endurance. It can run up to 50 kilometres per hour. Even at a trot foxes are speedy, at around 6 to 13 kilometres per hour.

When eating, say, a mammal or a bird, a fox will engage its impressive canine teeth and plunge its nippers into the neck, shaking or applying pressure until its prey dies. Sometimes it may use its teeth to disembowel the animal, possibly in two stages, first, applying pressure with its molars, before clamping its jaws down in one 'grinding, unrelenting crunch', as David Macdonald describes it.

Foxes also use their vibrissae, the sensory whiskers on their faces, when hunting. These large, useful hairs have follicles with blood-filled sinus tissues, connected to the sensory part of the brain, which help the fox as it lopes through undergrowth, particularly in poor light, alerting it to its environment and guiding its killing bites. The vibrissae can move rapidly back and forth and this allows the fox, a relatively small predator compared with others in the order *Carnivora*, a greater volume of space to sample. Proportionally, the fox's whiskers are longer than those of many other mammals.

The fox's senses are finely attuned to hunting. An animal that's active day and night – mostly hunting when the sun has set – must have eyes that work well in both light and dark. The fox can control the amount of light that passes through the lens of its eye to an impressive degree. In the dark, the pupil is large and round, but in bright light it is a vertical slit, similar to the pupil of a cat's eye. Beneath the light-sensitive cells it has a secret weapon called the tapetum lucidum, a layer of connective tissue that allows it to see much better in the dark, providing twice the amount of light that would be available normally. When a bright light, such as a spotlight or headlight, shines in a fox's eyes, they glow a kind of eerie green colour. If you are as still as a stone in front of a fox, like many mammals it may not be able to see you, but as soon as you make a move, it will know you're there.

The vulpine sense of smell is acute. Foxes use scent to locate animals underground; they can smell a mammal as far as a metre below the surface. They use this excellent sense of smell alongside the ability to hear high frequencies. Humans can pick up an average of 22,000 acoustic vibrations per second (hertz) at best, but foxes can hear well beyond the human range, picking up sounds up to 65,000 hertz. They can also hear at a range of up to almost 50 metres.

Once a fox has identified its prey, it can pinpoint the tiny movements of, say, a field vole and pounce with incredible accuracy. You may have seen the phenomenon in the wild, or on television. A fox is looking for food on a wintry day on a patch of land covered by deep snow. It pauses, twitches its ears – which can move independently of each other – and stands calmly, swaying, before suddenly tensing up, dropping down and springing all the way into the air in a 'mouse pounce', then diving into the snow head and paws first, its hind legs and bushy tail vibrating, snow flying everywhere as if the fox had jumped into a packet of icing sugar, before it emerges triumphant with a mouse in its jaws.

It's not just the sound and smell of prey that the fox is sensing. Between 2008 and 2010, scientists in the Czech Republic and Germany observed eighty-four foxes hunting and catching prey with the mouse-pounce technique. The foxes were more successful if they jumped on their prey while facing towards the north. Attacks from other directions were mostly unsuccessful and the results were the same regardless of time of year, day, cloud cover, wind direction, or age and gender of the fox.

It looked as though the foxes were using magnetic fields as an aid to hunting. The scientists suggested that the foxes were sensing the magnetic northerly direction as a patch of dark or light and using it to estimate the distance of the rodent. A protein called cryptochrome in the retina of the eye allows some animals, such as certain species of birds, to see the earth's magnetic field. Putting a blindfold on a robin, for example, will confuse its compass. It was already known that some animals – pigeons, bats, naked mole-rats, ants, lobsters, worms – used the earth's magnetic fields to navigate, but if the theory is correct, it will make the fox the first known animal to use these magnetic fields to hunt prey.

mamal

As an animal with such an impressive set of predatory tools, it seems that the fox wouldn't have any trouble taking down a lamb. But how much foxes eat lambs is a controversial topic about which it's impossible to be entirely sure. Varied though their diet is, they're not completely without discernment: apparently, some foxes find bank voles and shrews disgusting, and most do not like lamb fat, so lambs are not a preferred food for foxes. Macdonald writes that many foxes find them distasteful, his Niff included, and lamb carcasses can build up uneaten around fox dens.

Taste preferences aside, another reason foxes don't eat lambs is because other foodstuffs are easier to find and require less energy to hunt and kill. There's also the matter of access: farmers have improved their husbandry over the years and many now also lamb indoors. On the hard hills of Scotland, foxes kill just one in every fifteen to twenty lambs that die each year. On the Isle of Mull, where there are no foxes, lamb survival was no better than on the nearby mainland where foxes lived and were hunted.

Lamb has been found in their scat, so clearly it does form part of their diet – at least occasionally. But, as Roger Burrows wrote in his *Wild Fox: A Complete Study of the Red Fox*, the crux of the fox problem is this: how much of the fox's food is actually hunted, and how much of it is carrion – dead meat to be eaten later? Foxes are certainly scavengers, and farmers have reported foxes taking stillborn lambs, but when lamb is found in a dead fox's stomach, it is hard to say whether the lamb had already died of other causes. One farmer told me that he knows that a fox has taken a stillborn lamb if the entire body has been carried off; if it's just been pecked at, it may be gulls or another species of bird. Macdonald suggests the great majority of lambs eaten by foxes are already dead. Other predators, such as dogs, will also kill lambs, and sometimes foxes are blamed for these attacks. According to one of the world's leading fox experts, Professor Stephen Harris of the University of Bristol, foxes seen around lambing fields are much more likely to be looking for carrion than trying to catch live lambs. If the lamb is already dead, that doesn't pose such a problem for the farmer.

The Burns Inquiry, a government committee set up in 1999 to examine all the issues around the debate about hunting foxes with hounds, published its report in 2000. It contained accounts from a number of farmers who felt that hunting helped to protect their lambs, and without it, they would see an increase in the number killed by foxes. The report also looked at a study, carried out by the Game Conservancy Trust between 1995 and 1997, of the total reported pre-weaning losses that were blamed on foxes. In mid-Wales, for lambs born indoors and out, the figure was 3,134 out of 522,422 lambs (0.6 per cent). For outdoor lambs alone, the figure rose slightly to 1 per cent. The total regional loss of income would have been just under £100,000, spread across a number of farms. 'Of course, the effect of the loss on an individual farmer will vary, depending on his or her circumstances,' said the report.

For perspective, in 1998, the Ministry of Agriculture, Fisheries and Food estimated that farmers in Britain lose around 4 million lambs per year, out of approximately 16 million born, the value of the losses adding up to around £120 million. Deaths 'due to misadventure and predation' caused just 5 per cent of those deaths. Ultimately, the Burns Inquiry report surmised that less than 2 per cent of healthy lambs are killed by foxes in England and Wales with the caveat that 'levels of predation (or perceived predation) can be highly variable between farms and between different areas.' Usually in the lowlands, for example, lambs will be kept indoors, so the figures will be much lower.

Of course, even though it's rare, it must be very upsetting to lose a lamb. I recall the story of a local farmer near where my grandfather farmed in Scotland whose lambs' heads were apparently bitten off by foxes. As the story was passed through the family, it was said that one of the lambs carried on walking around for a while without a head, which somehow made the culprit seem that much more monstrous.

From some farmers' point of view, foxes do have an impact on their flocks. Veteran fox hunter Brian Fanshawe wrote submissions for the Burns Inquiry. In 2014, he gathered testimonies with writer Charlie Pye-Smith for his book *The Facts of Rural Life*. The stories they heard suggested that fox predation on lambs raised by Welsh farmers had increased since the Hunting Act had come into effect in 2005. One farmer, called Arthur Davies, said in one month in 2012, a lamb was killed every night, and that hunting was the best way of targeting problem foxes. In 2013, a survey was carried out on farmers in Wales, and, according to *BBC Wildlife* magazine, nearly all of them (96 per cent) had suffered financially as a result of foxes killing their lambs, and 75 per cent of them claimed there had been an increase in predation since the hunting ban had come into effect.

However, not everyone believes that lamb predation is as much of a problem as people make out. Richard Bowler is one of them. 'We wildlife photographers spend hours [outside], and I've never seen a photo of a fox attacking a lamb. If it's that common, show me a picture of a fox attacking a lamb. If someone did have that photo, it would be out there.'

And there are those in the farming community who do agree with him. One farmer I spoke with said that fox predation on lambs is largely a 'red herring'. Another, Rebecca Hosking, farms on the coast of South Devon. The day we spoke she'd been checking her sheep, making sure their toes were healthy going into winter. It had been a rainy morning but the weather was clearing up. Rebecca took over Village

Farm in March 2014. It has a stunning position, with views overlooking Salcombe, the estuary and the ocean, but its topography makes it challenging to protect the pastures from the elements, and the soil wasn't in the best condition.

Rebecca's ethos is regenerative and radical: she is working to turn the farm into a landscape that produces high-welfare food while also being a haven for wildlife. For her, the two aren't mutually exclusive. In the logo for Village Farm, a woman in a sailing boat, her mane of hair flying in the breeze, sits with a ram, a bird, a tree and, tellingly, a fox.

That's right: Rebecca is a sheep farmer who actively welcomes foxes onto her land. She told me she had 400 ewes and did her lambing outside but had foxes in the hedge right beside them. 'We don't get foxes taking healthy lambs,' she said.

Foxes are actually a huge benefit to Rebecca's farm because they keep the number of rabbits down. Seven rabbits eat the equivalent of the food required by one ewe. If the rabbit population booms, the production of lambs is affected. And a rabbit population boom could bring myxomatosis to the farm.

'It makes far more ecological sense for us as sheep farmers to have a healthy fox population,' she explained. 'We don't intervene at all. We don't shoot our rabbits or foxes or touch our badgers; we just let them balance.'

David Macdonald calculated that during its lifetime each

fox was worth between £156 and £886 to a farmer through reduced losses due to rabbit grazing. In some areas rabbits are the worst pest, feeding enthusiastically on a number of crops, from wheat and oats to potatoes and carrots. Foxes often catch rabbits in the countryside, you may even have been lucky enough to see one: the fox lowering its body close to the ground and creeping, slowly, stealthily, through the grass, until the moment is right and it breaks into a sudden gallop and launches itself onto its unlucky victim.

The agricultural method used at Village Farm is also likely to deter the foxes living on the land. To mimic a wild herd in nature, Rebecca grazes her animals in a tight group, which moves every day. Pigs and goats are in there too, which makes it less of an attractive proposition to a predator. It's a brilliant defence: the fox would have to be brave to take on a group of farm animals.

Only once has Rebecca come across a lamb eaten by a fox – she could tell because the bite of a fox is clean and precise and it has incisors on the side – but she happened to know on this occasion that this one had been born premature and was already dead. Rebecca also told me that foxes don't like lanolin or sheep fat unless they've no alternative, that they much prefer beetles or rodents, worms or rabbits, which is in line with Macdonald's and Harris's observations.

Rebecca knows a great deal about foxes because she rescued and lived with a fox throughout her twenties. A local woman was rearing a fox cub with kittens and Rebecca, a budding photographer and soon-to-be BBC documentary filmmaker, paid a visit to take some photos. The cub was starting to get big and bumptious, picking up the kittens by the neck and swinging them around the kitchen. Rebecca left the house with more than some snaps, and she kept 'Red' for six years. It was a catalyst for profound change in her family, who had previously been keen supporters of hunting.

One of the reasons the fox as hunter gets so much negative attention might have more to do with human behaviour. According to Defra's 2012 policy on the safe disposal of dead animals, farmers must remove 'fallen stock' (anything that dies on lowland farms) quickly to keep conditions sanitised and to avoid infection. Bodies can't be burned or buried; they must be swept up and frozen until a bag load is ready for the knackerman, who charges about £80 a bag to get rid of them. Some farmers, Rebecca said, would throw lambs to the foxes and write them off as killed by foxes to avoid paying for their removal: 'The fox gets collared and demonised for it, but I can see that that's exactly what happens.'

Where foxes get a particularly bad reputation is not over lambs but chickens. Birds make up a part of the fox's diet and lots of smaller, free-range holdings can be vulnerable to fox predation. It must be traumatic to walk out in the morning to collect your own eggs and be met with Parsley and Blossom with their heads ripped off, especially for the growing number of people keeping chickens as part of a sustainable lifestyle, often in urban areas. I have a vivid early memory of the shock, annoyance and sadness on a day when my grandmother lost her hens and lots of chicks to a fox who managed to break into a stable. They were a much-loved part of the wider animal family and I remember many afternoons spent collecting seashells from the beach for their calcium feed. Luckily, I didn't see the aftermath; it must have been distressing to find the bloody remains of those small chicks, so newly hatched. No wonder that people who've had their chickens – or a pet, which happens rarely – taken by a fox may often feel less inclined to support the fox.

The image that doesn't help the fox's cause is that, if it gets into a henhouse, it may end up killing a number of chickens and leaving their bloody, ripped-apart corpses in the coop, leading to the assumption that the fox has gone on some kind of psychotic Patrick Bateman-esque murdering spree – that it kills for fun.

There are two reasons for what it's doing. The first is called surplus killing, a behaviour that is common in above 200 of the species in the order *Carnivora*. It happens in the wild when a predator is faced with abnormal behaviour in its prey, such as birds nesting in the wrong place. It's a little like when we're met with a box of chocolates: even if our bodies don't need the sugar or calories, we may indulge in more than a couple.

The second is the fox's tendency to cache any surplus food. It is a great hoarder and will bury all kinds of food, from rodents to birds to frogs and rabbits, to eat at a later date either by itself or to feed its family. The fox isn't fussy about best-before dates or a bit of soil and sometimes the food will sit in a cache for several days. Interestingly, this behaviour requires the fox to remember where the hoard is and find it again, and it has been shown that foxes are able to do just that. An experiment conducted by Macdonald found that Niff was homing in precisely on her hoard, suggesting she remembered exactly where it was left instead of just hopefully looking in places where a cache might turn up. When you see a fox wandering through a country field with a mouse or rabbit hanging out of its mouth, it is probably looking for somewhere to stash it for later.

Foxes will cache their food thoroughly so they are also much more likely to find it again than another wandering mammal – apart from other foxes, who may have got there already, dug up the cache and eaten the meal for themselves. As a preventative measure, if they see another fox wandering near their treasure, they will remove the food once the coast is clear and take it somewhere else to reduce the risk of robbery. In areas where foxes and wolves still live together, foxes have been seen stalking wolves to see where they've hidden their cache, with plans to tuck in without having to expend energy on the tiring work of finding and killing.

Macdonald was lucky enough to see one of the foxes he tracked unearth a cache of a rabbit and he recorded it in his book. He describes the fox 'shaking and licking the flesh, eating bite by bite, sawing down the remains of the backbone to the pelvis, and crunching into the tops of the heavy leg bones'. For this meal, nothing was wasted.

So when a fox kills more than one chicken in a coop, it usually returns intent on burying the rest of the food, which it will keep doing until all the birds are taken away. Farmers will set up a gun near the coop to kill the fox, because they know that the fox will be back to collect another bird for its cache.

Although we can never know what or how a fox feels, 'fun', as we perceive it, is an inappropriate assumption. 'For pleasure, an animal will obviously kill because of the positive feedback of having successfully got food and being able to eat,' said Dr Dawn Scott of the University of Brighton. 'Foxes will kill more than they can eat at that period of time because they cache. Because they're opportunistic, if there is a chance to take more, they will take more, and kill multiple times, take those animals and go and cache them to store for other periods. In the same way that we fill up our larder, they fill up theirs.'

The chicken coop itself is an artificial environment. 'That scenario would never happen in the wild,' said Dawn. 'Humans have put it into an artificial scenario where that animal is exposed to multiple stimulus and the predatory responses are going to kick in. To not kill an animal that is flapping around goes against its innate behaviour to kill. It is just natural for that process to happen.'

Roger Burrows also makes an apt comparison: why don't we question why a lion kills a zebra, which he cannot possibly eat completely, when a small antelope would do? The fox, the lion, all other predators, kill and eat what they can. It's up to humans to take measures to protect their livestock.

Chris Packham feeds the foxes that live near him, but far away from the house so they don't become tame, and has an electric fence that protects his chickens. He hasn't had any losses in seven years. Likewise, Brian May, the animal welfare activist and Queen rock star, had a similar experience at the wildlife charity he was involved with, Harper Asprey Wildlife Rescue. 'We often have rescue ducklings, and we are well able to protect them from foxes; we never lose them,' he wrote to me. 'So any claim from farmers that it's impossible to make cages that those fierce foxes cannot break into, and livestock cannot be protected from predation, must be taken with a pinch of salt.'

While Richard Bowler has sympathy for people who've lost pets or chickens to a fox, the blame lies, he said, with the human: 'You're an intelligent human being; you can build something that's going to protect your animals. They [foxes] shouldn't be in there anyway because we should look after our chickens better than that.'

At Village Farm, with so many foxes around, Rebecca takes special precautions to look after her chickens, with an electric enclosure. Recently, the batteries stopped working and she lost the chickens to a fox. Initially she griped and moaned but then her fellow farmer reminded her, '*You* gave your chickens to the fox.'

'Chickens aren't native to this country,' she said. 'We domesticated one of the most dopey animals that sits there and lays eggs with no protection. So when a wild animal comes in, it's the same as saying "don't eat a doughnut" that is sat in front of us.'

She put the clash between foxes and some farmers thus: 'People like control. There's a lot of control in people's lives. Farming is: obliterate everything else bar the stuff you want. It's totalitarian. Look at it and step back: foxes really are our biggest and last predator in this country. We've knocked out lynx, wolves, sea eagles. Poor little foxes and badgers are the last bastion. People like control over things. People hate having foxes poo in their garden and [think] they're scum for doing that. They think, I must have control over my empire, my space.'

Of course, it can be upsetting when a fox does get in – and, despite precautions being taken, that can happen. Dr Alastair Leake of the Game & Wildlife Conservation Trust (GWCT) had just lost his chickens to a fox for the third time when we spoke. Leake's pen was about half an acre with a 7-foot-high fence, concreted all along the bottom so the foxes couldn't dig underneath – but they still managed to find a weak spot in the netting and pull it apart to squeeze through.

However, despite the nuisance, he didn't blame the fox or paint it as a villain. 'It can't help being a fox; it's only doing what's in its nature,' he said.

While foxes can't get near the industrial units that are more commonly used for meat production these days, the fox's behaviour in the chicken coop has profoundly affected its reputation. But it is foolish to judge a fox as we would a human. It is a wild animal and attributing intention or traits such as malice, revenge or psychopathy to it is a nonsense.

However, knowing that the fox's behaviour is natural isn't going to help someone whose chickens have all been killed feel any happier. The fox's refined predatory skill often clashes with human interests to such a degree that people try to control fox populations, using a variety of different methods – and with varying degrees of success.

3

To Catch a Fox

If the fox in the chicken coop surrounded by feathers and licking its lips with a malevolent smile is an iconic image, so too is what usually happens next: the fox in the crosshairs of the gun of a frustrated, red-faced farmer, bent on revenge and determined to protect his poultry.

The subjects of wildlife management and culling are complex, controversial and divisive, full of schisms, disagreements, opinions, agendas and conflicting studies. The beliefs and needs of those who live off the land and rely on the struggling rural economy often conflict with those of conservationists, which may also clash with those of gamekeepers, who look after shooting estates. It is not simple.

When it comes to foxes, it is especially complex. First, there is little consensus over whether any control is needed in the first place: to what extent are foxes a pest, a nuisance to shooting pursuits, a menace to other wildlife? Even if they are any of those things, does it follow that we should be trying to control their numbers? Do our attempts even have an effect? If so, how should we go about controlling them? What are the most humane methods? Questions such as these keep the debate very much alive. And the conversation can be extremely spirited.

One Thursday afternoon in October all hell broke loose on the Facebook page of Urban Fox Defenders. Hackney Council in East London was planning to kill a number of foxes that had set up home in the deer enclosure of Clissold Park. Online activists were posting calls to action across Facebook and Twitter, encouraging other fox fans to call the council and complain. A petition set up online received 400 signatures in less than an hour. The next morning it had almost 5,000 people making the effort to digitally state their opposition to a cull.

A statement eventually appeared on the Hackney Council website. 'The Council installed a large fence around the deer enclosure a number of years ago to protect the deer, but unfortunately the foxes have managed to get into the enclosure where they have made a number of earths (burrows). We have been advised by our independent deer expert that, living so closely together, they pose a hazard to the health of the deer.' It explained that the rubbish the foxes might bring in could cause ill-health or even death to the small population of fallow deer in the council's care. Deer could even break their legs by stepping on the foxes' earths. Instead, the foxes would be trapped and humanely killed.

The main argument of the petition – and of the RSPCA

– was that a cull would be pointless. 'Culling these animals is unlikely to accomplish anything as the territory will then be left vacant and it is likely that another group will move in instead. Foxes rarely interact with humans or deer,' the animal charity told the local *Hackney Gazette*.

As the volume of signatures on the petition rose, the reasons given in the comments became more and more emotional, from people all over the country. 'This is disgusting in a so-called civilised society!' 'This looks like a blatant attempt to justify bloodlust and must be stopped!!' 'Humans are the evil ones here.' 'Foxes are being deliberately vilified in an overt strategy to reintroduce the barbaric practices of the fox hunt.' 'DO NOT MURDER THE WILDLIFE.'

An hour after the council tweeted its intentions, another message appeared: 'In light of recent concern, we have removed fox traps from Clissold Park deer enclosure till further notice. Full update tomorrow.' The cull was postponed amid further discussion with the RSPCA and other fox advocate groups.

The following week, a leviathan street-art mural of a fox cub and a badger appeared in Walthamstow, close to the nature reserve where I walk. The badger cub sat behind a sign that read 'No to the cull', the fox next to a sign that read 'For Fox Sake', looking upwards at bees buzzing overhead. The artist, Louis Masai Michel, chooses animal subjects for his work to highlight environmental issues. For a couple of years his focus had been on endangered species, but the mention of a repeal of the Hunting Act around the 2015 general election drew his attention to the fox. 'I don't have much love for the government,' he said the day after he finished the piece. 'Since they've come to power they've created the badger cull, raised the idea of lifting the fox [hunt] ban and neglected to take any action against GMO and other things affecting the population of all pollinators, not just bees.' This aggravated the artist to the point of wanting to put out a message to the locals in east London.

It was a striking mural and I stood and stared at it for a while. It was also a stark reminder of the difference between cultures in urban areas and the countryside. I wondered, if Louis's mural had been painted in some areas of the countryside, how long it would have taken before a petition was raised for its removal. On the way back through the marshes, I listened for the cries of disturbed roosting birds that would give away the presence of a predator. A heron groomed and scratched its beak before crumpling down for a morning snooze. A skein of geese flew above, almost clipping my head as I stood on Wilson's Hill; I heard the machinery of their wings: up, down, up, down. I passed the canal boats with their poetic names: Therapy, Destiny, Barley, Wandering Jack, Roamin', and heard the gentle burble of a Hasidic Jewish man's morning prayers. Mist from the River Lea mingled with wood-smoke from the boats, dwellers making coffee. A friend sent a picture of a young-looking cub that liked to lie on the roof in the early sun each morning and fall asleep. That was my lot that day.

One question often brought up in the debate on population control is whether the number of foxes in Britain is increasing. It is hard to know exactly whether that is the case, as nationwide figures before the late 1990s were estimated using the National Gamebag Census, showing the numbers of foxes killed on shooting estates, which wasn't reliable for evaluating the population figures as a whole. Foxes also colonised new areas, such as Norfolk, and various British towns and cities after the Second World War, which raised their visibility, leading to the impression that fox populations were on the rise. Population densities are much higher in cities: in the countryside, on average, there are about two foxes per square kilometre, whereas in Bristol up to 37 foxes per square kilometre were recorded in the nineties, so you're much more likely to see them in urban areas. However, it is generally agreed that, due to increased availability of food, the fox population did grow in Britain through the twentieth century, stabilising in the 1990s.

These days, fox numbers seem to be steady. The population is estimated to be around 225,000 in rural areas and 33,000 in urban areas, which tots up to a total of 258,000 foxes across Britain. However, fox populations change throughout the year. Around 425,000 cubs are born each spring, leading to the illusion that there are suddenly more foxes around, but most of these won't survive their first year. In autumn they also tend to be more visible at the height of dispersal when they're wandering around looking for a mate or a breeding den. It's a natural waxing and waning of population. Sandra Reddy of the Fox Project, a charity dedicated to the protection of, rescue of and advocacy for the wild fox, believes it is the most widely misunderstood thing about foxes, particularly by the media: that fox numbers do change over the year, and that, overall, this doesn't equate to an increasing population.

Foxes breed once a year, in January and February. It is a small window: the vixen is on heat for three weeks but there are only three days of potential fertile mating. While the cubs grow in her womb, for about fifty-two days, the vixen will begin looking for a nest, or breeding earth. Lots of fox litters are raised under garden sheds, in banks, in flower-beds, under tree roots, piles of wood and rubbish, among tiles, on roofs or even in trees. There are usually four to five cubs in a litter (up to fourteen has been recorded, but that is rare). The vixen has six teats so is unable to feed more than six cubs at a time.

Cubs aren't the normal red, rust colour of foxes; they're a treacle brown, fluffier and softer, and, quite simply, adorable, which surely leads to the ill-advised desire to keep foxes as pets. They do bear some similarities to our domestic cats and dogs, particularly the former, oddly enough, as the two are not related. The vertical slit of the fox's pupils is feline, and not found in canines. Both cats and foxes can creep and prowl, with their bodies low to the ground, and leap on fences or trees at an impressive height. You never see a dog doing that, even though the fox is its close relation. The fox pounces and stalks like the cat, too. It's what is called convergent evolution – two genetically unrelated animals evolve similar traits to achieve the same end, in this case to hunt rodents and other small animals.

Despite the similarities to our more usual pets, as wild animals, foxes are not suited to living in a home. Accounts of those who've done it are full of stories of foxes chewing up almost anything they can get their teeth or sharp claws into and making a racket. It may be tempting to keep a pet fox, especially the delightful cubs, but it's not fair on the animal – and you'll probably have fewer friends wanting to come over because of the smell.

The cubs' eyes are closed at birth, but when they open they will turn from blue to fiery amber and their fur will redden and grow coarser. In the early days they need round-the-clock care from their mother, who provides contact heat to maintain their body temperature. The dog fox, their father, will bring food for them to eat once they're ready for solids, after a few weeks. Sometimes the vixen will eat food and regurgitate it for her cubs.

The fox's social structure is much more complicated than was previously realised. It's often assumed that foxes are solitary beasts, joining up only to mate. In fact, foxes live in very social, interdependent groups that aren't always the conventional 2.4 family set-up. The basic skulk, or family group, is made up of the parents and cubs, but often there will be a couple of non-breeding vixens in the group. Generally cubs from previous years or blood relatives, they are lower in the hierarchy than the breeding vixen, but will also look after the cubs as if they were their own.

Within the skulk the dynamic is mostly friendly and supportive. They keep in contact using scent and sound, meet during their wanderings and play together during the day. Cubs play-fighting are a delightful sight. They will roly-poly, bound and leap around, their squidgy, malleable-looking bodies all squashy with puppy fat and downy fur. Using their mouths, they will tentatively explore the motion of biting, often teeth-to-teeth with another sibling, but rarely doing any harm. They will dash and dart, learning how to react quickly to another cub's moves, skipping and hurling their bodies around a grassy play mat and testing each other's reflexes and reactions. Sometimes they will simply chase each other, often stepping on tummies and legs, the tiny white tips of their tails trailing like ribbons behind them, until they gain purchase and can tickle and nibble and nip and nose while the vixen grooms herself beside them, occasionally looking on to check everything's all right – it's a joyful scene. David Macdonald records watching a vixen somersaulting with a young cub and once saw eleven foxes playing together, which must have been a wonderful thing to witness.

When the weather starts to warm and the cubs become physically stronger, it is their time to go out and learn to find food. The vixen will encourage and teach them how to select and find different foods until they're big and knowledgeable enough to look after themselves. By September, the cubs have reached full size and can fend for themselves. Every autumn, the family dynamic will alter, as the young cubs disperse to find their own territories and mates.

Many cubs, however, won't reach this stage. Fox populations can sustain more than a 60 per cent annual mortality, and only a minority of foxes survive their first years – almost all will die before their fourth birthday. In captivity they can reach fourteen to fifteen years, but in the wild, the average life span is just eighteen months. So although the population increases dramatically at breeding time, the numbers soon fall back to pre-breeding levels.

In urban areas, foxes are killed for simple reasons: they're digging up or fouling lawns, ransacking rubbish, scaring residents or making a noise. The vixen's scream is famously disliked. Even if you don't regularly feed or even see a fox in a town or city, you have probably heard it. It will certainly be familiar if you live in a built-up area. It's that high-pitched, haunting, ghoulish wail that bounces from house to house, sounds like a baby being brutally bludgeoned to death in the woods and makes you wonder whether you should call 999 just in case. In fact, it's probably a romantic call from the vixen to the dog fox. Many people hate it, some love it, but, whichever way you stand, it is one of the most unearthly sounds of the British landscape. Hearing it in the dead of night can be quite chilling. You can picture the fox tilting back its head and opening its jaws wide to emit the loudest possible call; the eerie howl of the wolf's smaller, orange cousin.

Dr Nicholas Newton-Fisher of the University of Kent has studied fox vocalisations and explained more about the vixen's scream. 'We found this call was high-pitched, with a long duration and continuous sound which suggested a contact call. The longer a call goes on the longer the animal has to locate it.' He compared it with a phone ringing and ringing until you find it. 'It's the same principle with animal vocalisation, it makes it easier for them to be located.'

The vixen's scream is just one of twenty-eight different calls that can be split between contact and interaction calls. Contact calls vary with distance, whereas interaction calls vary with aggression. Foxes have multiple vocalisations, all with different structures and frequencies, suggesting that they have a complex language and way of communicating with each other.

Nick was surprised by how many calls the fox had compared with, say, a dog, which 'can just bark, whine and shriek'. Also, individual foxes have different voices. 'A call could be a signature of an individual; it could relate to body size, could relate to intent, or the emotional state of the animal.'

Other sounds include a stuttering, throat-based noise, one or two explosive barks or the dog-like 'wow wow wow' which translates as meaning something like 'Hello, I'm here, where are you?' The sharper calls are warning calls to sound an alarm or to communicate aggression. The clicketing call with fast bursts of sound strung together is also associated with aggression.

Foxes make more calls in winter, during the mating season. The famous shriek is not, as the myth goes, a result of pain caused by the barbed penis of the male. It's difficult to be sure exactly what it means, but it's a way of the vixen identifying her location, possibly to encourage the dog fox to come hither. 'I've seen a few foxes do it, and they're not lying on the ground in pain,' said Nick.

So foxes are capable of making a lot of noise and, for some people, that's enough to want to get rid of them. In the past, councils would often arrange for the culling of these foxes, but that doesn't tend to happen any more. However, it's still perfectly legal for anyone to hire a pest-controller with the requisite firearm licence privately, and foxes are routinely culled in London and other cities in Britain.

Foxes annoy people. I already knew this because I'd read about it, although I'd never actually met anyone who really cared, let alone cared enough to pay to have them killed. The foxes around where I live occasionally make noises but it had never bothered me in the slightest. Our rubbish is kept in lidded bins, our tortoise safe inside and we don't have a proper garden, just a raised terrace. I loved the times I'd spotted them, and longed to see them more.

But, it turns out, the practice of shooting foxes is more widespread than I had imagined. Bruce Lindsay-Smith has been in the business of pest control for decades and has killed a lot of foxes, thousands by his estimation, more foxes than an average hunt over the last thirty years. He wouldn't be drawn on the total number, but did say that he had killed thirty foxes in Dartford, thirteen in two hours in a back garden in New Malden and thirty-five on a golf course in one night. Local authorities' nationwide stance not to control foxes hadn't made much of a dent in his work.

When Bruce was a toddler in the 1960s, he remembers staring out at the freezing night sky and at a field covered in sheep and snow. He saw a black dot moving along the field perimeter, which turned out to be a fox, and then he saw his dad with a gun, hunting the animal. He found out that his dad had shot the fox, but not before it had already killed two lambs, apparently. 'Things like that stick in your mind for ever,' said Bruce. It was an important and formative moment in the development of his psyche and influenced the direction of his life.

The pest-control business has changed quite a bit over the last thirty years or so. Bruce started working for Bexhill and Henley Rabbit Clearance Society and then Rentokil. In those days there were few pest controllers in the phone directory. He had contracts with the government and made money on the side selling hundreds of fox skins. Now, fox corpses are sent off to be burned in an incinerator.

It's not a job everyone supports. Some of his traps have been broken in areas of London where he's worked – 'Nursing homes and hospitals where staff have said, "Oh, that's cruel, I'm not letting them trap the foxes"' – but he said his work was rarely disrupted.

Bruce allowed me to shadow him on a job to exterminate foxes at a mansion in South London, where the crime committed by foxes was fouling. 'There's fox mess everywhere and the stench of fox urine coming in under the floor. The man who lives there has young children and he just can't have this risk around.'

Under instruction, the housekeeper had put out food

every night for a week in the spot that would be the target of Bruce's rifle. He'd already been there to do a risk assessment and make sure it was safe to shoot in. He called the local police to tell them he'd be poking out of a window with a massive rifle, in case anyone panicked, 'and then you'd end up with the tactical firearms department turning up and kicking the front door in'.

It turned out, from what I heard, that the little girl had been feeding the fox, unbeknown to her mother or father. And Bruce acknowledges the human element is often to blame. 'People don't realise how much of a problem they're causing,' he said. 'Foxes thrive on man's bad habits and terrible waste systems, throwing rubbish around and food on the streets when they come out of the pub on a Saturday night, throwing stuff on the bird table. Some people don't even know they're doing it, putting food waste in a plastic bag outside the front door. A couple of scratches and the fox is in there with a meal.'

As Bruce set up his rifle, I began to feel a little queasy at the idea that I could witness the death of a fox, particularly as there might also be cubs. If so, Bruce would shoot these as well, his reasoning being that without the vixen the cubs would starve to death, which is, he said, a crueller way to die.

We waited and I peered into the garden with Bruce's special UV binoculars. We glimpsed a fox from the other side of the road and waited for it to enter the garden. He shared with me all the things he'd seen foxes do while we sat there. Swimming, walking along the top of a fence, walking across roofs, jumping off scaffolding. One litter of cubs lived on the seventh floor of the Royal London Hospital. 'Did you . . . get them?' I asked, not really sure how to put it. He nodded.

What he told me next, though, surprised me. One day he received a call from a Rentokil surveyor who said a fox cub was being stoned to death by builders on a building site in Romford, Essex. They asked Bruce to do something about it and he drove down. He arrived at the scene and saw a fox cub, so young and tiny it could fit inside a pint glass, lying in a ditch, being tortured by a group of men. It was completely in shock and terrified but still alive. People who worked in the building pleaded with him not to kill the cub. They were worried about bad publicity for the building site. Bruce gave them his word that he would take it to an animal rescue centre, rather than shoot it. 'It didn't seem to have had a fair start to its life,' explained Bruce.

But he didn't take it to a rescue centre; he took it home. Now the cub's fully grown and lives with him and his dogs. 'It used to play with the Labrador,' he remembered, 'jumping over its back. He's very shy. We go in there every day to give him a stroke, clean him out and feed him. We can't turn him out because he wouldn't know how to hunt.'

It is a profound example of the fact that people's relations with animals are usually a lot more complicated than you'd first imagine. Bruce kills foxes for a living but he doesn't loathe them at all. 'In no way be deliberately cruel or unkind to any animal,' he told me. 'Its life is as important to it as ours is to us; it's just that we human beings consider things rather than go on our instinct as such,' he said.

Back in the house, it was cold, and it had started to rain outside. We had been there for a few hours, it was coming on for 11 p.m., but no foxes had come into the garden. I left to catch my train home, secretly pleased to head off without seeing the kill. I texted Bruce the following day to thank him and ask what had happened.

The next morning I turned my phone on and some picture messages appeared. A fox lay motionless on the fake, expensive grass, blood around its body and smeared on the path. Its beautiful, black-edged tail was lifeless and pathetic. The other fox's face and head were covered in blood but its eyes were open. Stark, staring, dead. From another angle, I could see the shot of the first fox as crimson blood dripped down his white neck. Blood was smeared around the edge of the garden. I didn't know what to reply.

In rural areas, the situation is much more complicated, as there are many conflicting interests and reasons for controlling fox populations. Culling is most likely to happen where there are both game and agricultural interests. One landowner might cull foxes because they eat poults (baby pheasants or partridges), which curtails the weekly shoot if there aren't enough birds to go around. A farmer might want to wipe out any foxes to avoid potential predation on their lambs or poultry, or prevent the possible spread of disease. Another might simply enjoy killing the loathed vermin – and nail carcasses to a gate to make a point.

Around 80,000 foxes are shot each year by farmers and gamekeepers. There is no closed season; foxes of any age and sex can be killed throughout the year. A study on regional variation in fox management conducted by Matthew Heydon and Jonathan Reynolds of the GWCT (or the Game Conservancy Trust, as it was called at the time) sent questionnaire surveys to landowners and tenant farmers. Around half the farmers responded to the survey, and the results showed that fox culling was prevalent in each region (mid-Wales, the east Midlands and East Anglia). In fact, between 70 and 95 per cent of those farmers were involved in culling in some form. Both the reasons and methods varied between the regions, although the most common reason (67 per cent) was to minimise losses of livestock and game.

Andrew Cook, who'd been a Master of Foxhounds in Scotland since the mid-1990s, after agricultural college in

Cirencester, sees foxes as a pest species that needs control-ling. 'The rearing of game birds, lambing, chicken units – they're conflicting with lots of interests in the countryside.' He felt that the divide between urban life and the country-side meant that people misunderstood the problem of both foxes and badgers. City-dwellers might not understand the impact animals could have on livestock, and how upsetting or irksome it could be to find a lamb with its stomach or other organs removed by a fox or badger. 'People in a town couldn't possibly understand why the badger is a pain,' he said. As he spoke, his handsome pack of hounds bayed excit-edly – calls of 'ar-oooo' echoing around the stable buildings.

There is also an argument for wildlife management: controlling fox numbers in order to protect biodiversity. Some landowners might want to protect ground-nesting birds, such as skylarks or plovers, because they are a beloved part of rural life. These birds can roost in the trees, but once the hen has laid her eggs she needs to sit tight on the ground, and often finds herself in the path of a hungry predator. A nature reserve might want to pick off a couple of a hungry foxes to protect breeding waders, such as the oil-slick-feathered lapwing with its ostentatious mohican, or the curlew, with its wonderfully long and curved beak, or seabirds, such as the little tern, with its smart, monochrome head markings.

Even conservationists, the last people you might expect,

will admit that occasionally killing a small number of foxes in order to maintain specific species balance by protecting rare birds might be necessary. The broadcaster Chris Packham, for example, isn't completely opposed to controlling fox numbers for this reason, though he favours creative conservation (fences, other non-lethal deterrents) over destructive conservation (killing animals). 'We're talking about the need to necessarily farm rare birds because elsewhere there isn't an opportunity for them outside of these focused highly managed areas,' he said. But he argues that there's a fundamental difference between controlling foxes to produce and protect a greater crop of rare birds, such as avocets, redshanks and snipe, as the RSPB do, and gamekeepers controlling foxes to produce a greater number of pheasants and partridges, which are being bred only to be hunted for entertainment.

The GWCT supports the culling of foxes as a response to its own research and studies. It is a science-focused charity that aims for a thriving countryside rich in game and other wildlife. Dr Alastair Leake, Head of the Trust's Allerton Project, a centre for research into and education about rural affairs, has no doubt that 'without some form of fox control we would see an impact on biodiversity'.

From 1985, the Trust carried out an experiment across three sites, Salisbury Plain, Loddington in Leicestershire, and Royston in Hertfordshire, to study the impact of predator control – the killing of foxes, stoats, rats and other animals that prey – on the populations of hare, grey partridge and pheasant. At Loddington, the study found that periods of predator control as well as habitat improvements had led to higher brown hare densities, up to 78 hares per 100 hectares. When the gamekeeper stopped controlling predators from 2002, for comparison, hare density decreased significantly; by 2006 it was less than 10.

There are many other reasons why populations of brown hare and ground-nesting birds are vulnerable – agricultural changes, habitat loss, climate change – but the Trust concluded that, across all three sites, predator control was indeed a significant determinant of wildlife population. 'We are aware that killing predators is controversial. Some people say it is not necessary, but we believe otherwise,' Nick Sotherton, the Trust's director of research, told the *Guardian*.

The wider data on species decline is galling. Over the past half-century Britain has lost more than 44 million breeding birds, for example. We'll be lucky to see a lapwing or a cuckoo again. Some scientists believe a third of all bird species worldwide will be gone by the end of the century.

The fox is often called out as a predator of breeding and ground-nesting birds, but it is not necessarily the main culprit. It has had such a bad reputation for centuries in Britain that it is often accused of predation when, in truth, the main cause of death may be something else. Buzzards, for example, or poor husbandry, in the case of livestock. Rats, squirrels and other birds also prey on vulnerable British birds. The People's Trust for Endangered Animals say that fox predation isn't much of a factor in its work in protecting endangered species. One gamekeeper who controlled foxes to protect baby pheasants, bred for shooting, noted that not only had the fox population not changed considerably in the forty years he had been working the land, it was actually buzzards that were more of a predator on the poults he managed.

Brian May, hirsute guitarist, astrophysicist, animal welfare activist, is one of the most influential leaders of the pro-fox community. He has a large following on social media, and uses his platforms to talk about animal cruelty, particularly badgers and foxes.

'You need to look at the bigger picture; we are destroying habitats which in turn destroy the species that inhabit them – leaving endangered species in small isolated pockets,' he wrote to me. 'There is little point in increasing the numbers of a species if there is insufficient habitat to support them.

'The real reason for the decline of birds and other wild creatures can always be traced to human intervention. Lapwings and curlews coexisted with foxes for hundreds of years before their habitat was compromised by human activity. We have to look to our own behaviour to discover why the numbers have declined. The natural extinction rate of species on Earth has been recently estimated to have accelerated a hundredfold since Man became numerous as a species. So clearly the problem is us, but finding the solution is not so easy, especially in a culture that prioritises economic growth above any other consideration.'

So while foxes are a factor in the population of some species, they aren't the ultimate problem for diminishing wildlife. That's habitat loss and destruction, even in the last thirty years. Farmland birds started to decline markedly in 1975 and breeding waders followed, owing to a combination of agricultural drainage, the intensive use of fertilisers and habitat deterioration. Weather changes, too, are having an impact, with more pronounced wet and dry periods. Waders and ground-nesting birds were abundant in lowland England but are now concentrated in only a small number of sites, where they are vulnerable to predators as a result of the destruction of the habitat mosaic they require.

Brian was clear: we are the destroyers who need to change our behaviours – for example, our waste-disposal systems, which impact on the diet and health of foxes – to correct past mistakes. 'We need to stop controlling wildlife and start controlling ourselves,' he said.

It could be argued that attempts at population control are just another way humans blindly interfere with natural ecosystems, without knowing exactly what other knock-on damage could be caused. Prairie dogs, for example, have been controlled in the southwestern United States and are now a threatened species. That has had a crucial impact: too late, people realised that they were essential in maintaining the productivity of the grassland ecosystem, through loosening, turning and aerating the soil, like big earthworms. The grassland has now been largely destroyed.

The now extinct thylacine, or Tasmanian tiger, killed sheep and chickens brought into Australia by settlers and was killed for a bounty offered by the government. The cull was brutally effective and the last animal died in the 1930s. Darwin's fox was driven to the edge of extinction after settlers deemed it a livestock pest on the Falkland Islands – it is now classed as critically endangered, with those left in the wild, mostly in Chile, thought to number just over 300. The red fox is, of course, currently flourishing, but that doesn't mean its future is assured.

Whichever argument people use for controlling population numbers, the other question is whether culling is effective. There is very little consensus over whether it actually makes a difference to populations; studies and opinions vary greatly.

Culling is certainly not the main cause of death in foxes. About 80,000 are thought to be shot each year, but the most common way for a fox to die these days is from a traffic accident. In *Urban Foxes* Stephen Harris and Phil Baker reported findings of a sample of 1,000 fox deaths in Bristol. Most had died from train and car contact. The next most common deaths were through snares, disease and fighting. It is rare, but young cubs are also vulnerable to golden eagles, which have sharp talons. In some of the most jaw-dropping footage ever filmed for the BBC's *Winterwatch*, a red fox battles a golden eagle over a carcass in the Trossachs. As the fox approaches the meat it realises an eagle is already there, and lunges threateningly and aggressively. The eagle opens its enormous wings and beak wide and a dance ensues between the two, hopping towards each other to intimidate, ducking and diving to defend. The golden eagle jabs its wings like the kung fu master Bruce Lee while the fox seems to aim for its heart with whip-quick reactions, teeth bared and making a gekkering sound. In this incident the fox emerged victorious, but it is easy to see how a cub could become an unlucky victim.

The main disease that foxes suffer in Britain is sarcoptic mange. It is a horrible thing to contract, caused by a parasitic mite called *Sarcoptes scabiei,* which burrows into the fox's skin in great numbers and makes it incredibly itchy. Up close (very close – it is microscopic), the mite resembles a squished pin cushion with various appendages that look like needles. The lacerations and cuts caused by the fox's scratching leave it vulnerable to infection and it will usually die within four to six months from starvation, hypothermia or organ failure unless properly treated. A fox with mange looks ill, with patchy fur, encrusted sores on its skin, weight loss and infected eyes. Sarcoptic mange is also contagious and can be catastrophic for fox populations. In the 1990s, an outbreak of mange in Bristol wiped out 95 per cent of the city's foxes. Dogs and cats can also occasionally be infected with the mite, as can humans, though in the latter case the condition will clear up after a few weeks.

Another high-profile disease that foxes can carry is thankfully one that hasn't existed in Britain since 1902: rabies. Although it is less common in Europe than it is in Africa and Asia, one of the principal vectors is foxes, meaning that in many countries they are associated with the disease, which has led to fear and intensive culling (even though culling may make the situation worse by upsetting the dynamic of groups and territories, causing foxes to disperse in larger areas, and thus carry the disease further). Over the last three decades an oral vaccine has proved successful in eliminating fox-mediated rabies in vast areas of Europe.

Other diseases and parasites foxes can contract include the tapeworm *Echinococcus multilocularis*. It is found in much of the northern hemisphere but not Britain and it can be fatal to humans, who can catch it through ingesting fruit that might carry traces of fox faeces or through a domestic pet. According to scientists at Bristol University, lungworm

(*Angiostrongylus vasorum*) in dogs, cats and foxes is an increasing problem in Britain and elsewhere, although pets can be wormed and treated to avoid it becoming fatal. It is carried by slugs and snails, but often foxes are the animals blamed in stories in newspapers.

Aside from misadventure, culling and disease, foxes regulate their own numbers to a certain degree, because they are territorial animals, and the size of their territories is dependent on the availability of food. Simply speaking, if a vixen has, say, seven cubs, and there is not enough food in the territory to feed them all, a number of the cubs will die. If there is plenty of food, a greater number might survive. It is also thought that the non-breeding vixens can suppress their reproductive ability, either through behaviour (choosing to become the non-breeding nannies of the group and switching off scent receptors that signal they are available to local male foxes), or even by not producing eggs, aborting cubs or failing to rear them when born. While there are enough resources and food to go around, foxes will breed at a stable rate. If the availability of food increases, the population will do so too.

This also means that if foxes are killed on a territory with sustainable food sources, a new one, or group, will simply move in. Chris Packham believes that, because of this, controlling foxes works only in localised areas for temporary periods. Some studies have even suggested that fox culling can result in a slightly higher population as it can leave areas open to a higher number of itinerant foxes looking for new earths. Malcolm Brockless, the gamekeeper employed by the GWCT, told the *Guardian* he had killed an average of twenty-five adult foxes a year on the Loddington farm over three years. No neighbouring farms employed gamekeepers, so there was a constant flow of new foxes onto the now vacant territory. Another gamekeeper admitted that he didn't really know if culling worked; it wasn't clear if the number would rise if he stopped killing them.

There are conflicting studies on whether foxes regulate their own population, however. A computer experiment, conducted by Jonathan Reynolds, David Macdonald and others, modelled the impact of four methods of culling foxes in a large area (1,600 square kilometres): hunting with hounds, winter shooting, culling at the den and fertility control. They found that the most effective way of reducing fox populations was by culling at the den, taking out the mother and cubs. Shooting during the winter months also had an impact as it targeted the lone, wandering foxes, searching for new territories. However, these methods worked only at intensive levels, and so are only practical for smaller areas. Without solving the problem of the itinerant foxes filling the newly vacant territories, culling foxes did not work. Another study, of forests in upland Wales, also demonstrated that the number of foxes killed had no effect as they were being replaced by immigrating foxes.

On the other hand, a GWCT study by Heydon and Reynolds, accepted in 1999, showed very different results. Studying the three regions again, they found that fox populations in A and C were not self-regulating, that culling was a key factor in overall mortality in all three regions, showing a definite impact on fox density, and that it could decrease fox numbers both regionally and locally. They concluded that they 'believe it is a crucial conceptual step to appreciate the importance of human interference in determining the predator–prey relationships found in modern environments'. It is worth considering, however, that the research for the study was enabled by a contract from the Countryside Alliance.

Bruce Lindsay-Smith's impression is that when a fox is killed, its space will be filled, but not for a while. 'You will get other foxes come in but it might not be immediately and someone's place might be free of them for maybe two or three years before they get any further problems,' he said. However, on the issue of regular callbacks, he did also say that in certain areas the fox problem was ongoing. Clapham, he said, had the biggest problem with foxes. 'There are more callbacks in Clapham every year to deal with the same people's fox problems.'

Setting aside whether we should be controlling fox populations or not and how effective it is, the other contentious point is the most humane way to kill the animals.

In rural areas, foxes are shot (with a shotgun or rifle), snared, trapped, hunted and dug out from underground earths with or without terrier dogs. A fox caught alive must be killed humanely with a firearm. Lamping is a popular method for nocturnal predators such as the fox – a high-powered light is shone at the animal, stunning it and giving a few seconds of immobility in which it can be shot in good visibility. Like snaring, it is often carried out by gamekeepers, or in areas where wild or reared game is present.

For the GWCT, controlling foxes involves sophisticated planning. During the nesting season of birds such as skylarks, lapwings and meadow pipits, crops are at knee height so it is difficult to get a clean shot, Dr Alastair Leake explained. To solve the problem, his staff will rig up remote-control CCTV cameras on posts to record which routes the foxes are regularly using. Once a fox is seen using a tramline of a field regularly, a snare is placed down. The GWCT holds part-time gamekeeper's courses to improve the quality of the training.

The traditional idea of a snare is that of a noose that tightens around the neck as the animal attempts to escape. 'That might have been the case in Victorian and Edwardian times,' said Leake, 'but those snares were outlawed many years ago.' He was sure 'strangulation' snares were not used any more as they are illegal and therefore difficult to get hold of. As well as self-locking neck snares, leghold traps (gin traps), poison and gas are prohibited.

These days the only legal snare is a free-running snare, like the 'breakaway' snare designed by the Head of Predation Control Studies at the GWCT, Jonathan Reynolds. It has a stop on it, which means it cannot run all the way down until it is tight on the animal's neck. It is a long, thin, metal noose with a few fastenings. Once attached to a post on one of the fox's 'desire lines' or paths, with a loop hanging at around the height of a fox's head, the snare can catch the fox and keep him – it is usually a him; one gamekeeper told me vixens were cleverer at avoiding snares, maybe because they tend to be smaller and thus more mobile – until morning when he would be shot in the head. Legally, the snares must be checked every 24 hours, and with 400 across the estate the gamekeeper looked after, it was quite intensive work. He believed it to be the most humane way to control foxes and maintained that he had very rarely seen a snare go wrong and injure an animal.

Snares have their critics, though. The League Against Cruel Sports had called for a ban on their use, stating on its website that a snare 'silently garrottes its victims, and often leads to a painful and lingering death'. There is also a danger of bycatch – other animals getting caught in the snares – which is why the RSPB doesn't use them on its reserves.

Many opponents to killing foxes are open to other, non-lethal ways of controlling fox populations. Dawn Scott, for example, described the exercise of culling as creating a 'sink, where you end up killing and killing'. Instead of killing foxes, she said, we can control fox numbers by analysing and thinking about our own behaviour.

And there are alternatives out there. While many farmers and gamekeepers consider it worthwhile to cull, the situation in urban areas is different. Since the 1980s, the councils of Britain have mostly stopped culling, due to the efforts of Trevor Williams, one very determined fox-lover.

When he was seven years old, Williams worked the harvests at his uncle's farm in Hereford. It was his favourite place to go for holidays, so much so that he would throw a tantrum if the seaside won out over the farm one year. 'I loved the whole thing,' he remembered. 'I was fascinated by watching animals. Foxes, in particular. We were walking through the orchard one day and this fox jumped up from underneath the tree and in my mind even now I see fire. It was this vivid orange thing that rocketed away. That's vividly in my memory.'

Nature temporarily forgotten, Williams wanted to be a rock 'n' roll star, and he achieved his dreams for a while, playing in a band called Audience from 1969 to 1972.

Afterwards, he did session work but soon became jaded by the music industry. He began to loathe airports and hotels and longed to do something he felt was a bit more worthwhile.

His interest in the welfare of wildlife drew him to hunt sabotage, which was at the height of its activity in the 1970s. His first day out was a complete shock. He expected to be putting down repellants, spraying chemicals around or shouting rude words, nothing major. Instead, he found himself in the middle of a 'phenomenal' battle. 'We were putting down repellants, when from two sides this gang of thugs started lobbing rocks and sticks at us. I thought, this is amazing! This is like a war zone! I thought, I'm not having this, which made me commit to it.'

Not only did the experience draw him firmly into the HSA, it also pushed him into watching wildlife again, as he had done as a young child. Soon he was setting his alarm for 4 a.m. – 'something a musician never does' – and he'd find himself standing and watching out for signs of badgers. 'I soon found that badgers were boring and they were all the same. Foxes, though, were all entirely different, built differently, walked differently, with different personalities. Some serious, some fun-loving. They're dogs. They're fascinating.'

Trevor, John Bryant (his friend, the animal activist and founder of Protect Our Wild Animals) and a couple of others realised while they were sabbing in the late 1970s that there were more foxes being killed by local authorities than by hunts in Britain – tens of thousands of foxes per year – but it wasn't solving the problem. They wanted to do something about it.

The argument they put to the councils was that culling clearly wasn't working, so they were wasting public money on a fruitless task. 'It doesn't matter what you do, they'll breed back to the same numbers anyway,' said Trevor. They explained the science with a study of the fox population over a year comparing two councils that did nothing to control foxes – Lambeth and Southwark – with Lewisham, which he said had killed eighty-one foxes that year. Lambeth and Southwark had done nothing and their fox population had remained at the same level. But Lewisham's fox population was also the same at the end of the year, even though hundreds of pounds had been spent on the cull.

The pest controller's contract was terminated – although he got his own back on Trevor by post. 'We heard from the guy's dog, who sent us something in an envelope as thanks for losing them all their work, which was a small price to pay,' hooted Trevor. 'And a string of bad language, not that it was readable.'

Instead of killing foxes, Trevor wanted to deter them. Hunt saboteurs use repellents, bought from garden centres or pet shops, to undermine the scenting ability of the dogs.

Trevor figured that if they tried this on the fox's territory, they wouldn't be able to find food and it might act as a deterrent and move the foxes away.

The idea began to grow with funding from the League Against Cruel Sports. Trevor was a leading light in the hunt saboteur world and people trusted him. Bexley Council was the first to take him on officially, then Croydon, then Bromley, and it soon made sense for Trevor to leave the League and set up a fox consultancy. 'I had £400 and a narrow plan, to mail every council in the country saying I'm setting up a hotline for anyone who has problems with foxes. I'm working with different councils in the London area, I know you don't have to deal with foxes legally and you don't really know much about foxes, so this would be an opportunity to pass off work you don't have to deal with. I thought if I can double this, I can probably make a reasonable living. Within a fortnight I was working for sixty-five councils. Most of it was trying to solve people's problems by phone.'

Trevor also created a mailed questionnaire that people could fill out to customise the advice he was giving, and soon the organisation became a fox information bureau. At the time, in the 1980s, he was unhappy with the myths and legends about foxes that were propagated, that they killed for fun, or that they were completely harmless, for example. He realised that there wasn't enough factual information about foxes for people to draw their own conclusions, they were having to rely on information given by the two groups who had opposing interests in the matter, who he felt were using and interpreting the data in ways to suit their own arguments: the League was practically suggesting that foxes were vegetarians and wouldn't harm a chicken or a rabbit, while the British Field Sports Society, now the Countryside Alliance, would say foxes killed 11 million lambs a year. 'That was a figure they once used,' said Trevor, shaking his head with disbelief. 'A third of all lambs born!'

The rhetoric on both sides has changed now, with both sides relying more on facts and data, although there is still plenty of room for interpretation, with each side quoting the Burns Inquiry's report for its own ends. (The conclusions of the report were somewhat ambiguous and could be interpreted according to different agendas.) In part that is because there is more scientific data available, with an increased number of studies and research, aided by technological innovations such as infra-red cameras. The League also employs high-profile anti-hunt public figures in digital media, such as a video entitled 'Horror of Hunting – Celebrity Reactions', which sees Uri Geller, Tony Robinson, Bill Oddie and Gemma Atkinson react in shock to footage of a fox being hunted. The Countryside Alliance, on the other hand, emphasises pest control and wildlife management as reasons for hunting, and tends not to mention the recreational side quite as much.

In 1993, Trevor and his wife took in three injured foxes. Over the next ten years, he regularly found himself bottle-feeding cubs through the night. They had a fox refuge on their hands, and a new facet of the Fox Project quickly became the care of foxes.

Trevor retired in 2014 and handed the directorship over to Sandra Reddy. Even though the rescue work is a lot more visible on the Facebook page, particularly with photographs, the organisation still gives advice to almost every council in Britain and takes 6,000 calls a year from the public about getting rid of foxes. Although they take in 750 or so injured foxes a year, they're saving the lives of many, many more, on the quiet. 'Every call is one fox and that's the most important thing, still,' he said. 'People call to complain about a fox digging up the garden. Most say, "I don't want them killed, I just want the problem solved", even people who have a problem with foxes, more and more people don't want them killed. People don't want to kill something for nothing.'

The RSPB is another supporter of non-lethal control. Lots of wildlife in Britain is now concentrated in the small oases of nature reserves run by the RSPB, which tries to provide a healthy environment for birds and all wildlife in Britain. There are 214 of them, and they inevitably attract predators looking for food in the impoverished countryside. Working out what to do to protect animals was an extremely difficult question for the charity, whose starting point was always that it didn't want to kill anything. Species balance is perhaps the most complex, controversial and difficult task for an ecologist, particularly when there are so many fluctuating variables, from disease to weather changes, social pressures and rapid declines of population.

The sky was an opulent blue and the cold air felt pleasing on my cheeks as I walked through the RSPB headquarters at Sandy, listening to the frenetic song of the robin and keeping an eye out for the yellow stripe of a goldcrest's cap. Wizened blackberries and desiccated bracken bordered the paths. If it had been another hour, foxes would have been prowling through the undergrowth, looking for a tasty vole.

Graham Hirons (Chief Ecologist) and Gwyn Williams (Head of Reserves and Protected Areas) have over seventy years' experience of conservation between them. The method they look at first and foremost to keep foxes out is fencing. 'Anti-predator fences are the best way,' explained Graham. Lapwing nesting success, he said, is 78 per cent inside fences and 20 per cent outside. They also fence out foxes from islands in coastal lagoons and shingle banks, to protect breeding avocets and little terns. Since the early 2000s when the RSPB started using fencing, technology and design have improved and are now used on thirty-seven reserves. However, foxes are intelligent; they often find their way through the barriers. 'It's a bit of an arms race,' said Graham.

Other methods that have worked in the lab but not so well in the field are using scent, such as lion dung, to give the fox the idea there's a larger predator around, and aversive conditioning, which means training the fox not to eat what you don't want it to eat. An experiment by David Cowan, Jonathan Reynolds and Elaine Gill looked at reducing predation using conditioned taste aversion. Four captive foxes were given pheasant meat treated with an illness-inducing chemical. Two of the foxes vomited. A week later the foxes were given pheasant meat without any chemicals in it. They approached the meat but then retreated, 'shaking their heads', and didn't even taste it. This happened eight more times over a year, and they all reacted in the same way. It sounds as if it works but, said Gwyn and Graham, it is difficult to replicate in real life. Other ways of controlling fox behaviour include manipulating habitats, for example, leaving longer grass around the edge of the field so the fox will spend more time hunting rodents there.

If all else fails, they consider lethal control, but only between January and March. 'We are keen as an organisation not to leave orphan cubs so we stop fox control in March and anyone shooting after that date needs special dispensation,' said Gwyn. In 1989, the RSPB controlled foxes on just a 'handful' of estates. From April 2014 to September

2015, 28 reserves killed 412 foxes (out of a total 37 reserves that had permission to do so).

The efficiency of culling varies according to area. In the uplands, for example, the intensity of control means the number of animals able to occupy a new territory is few, thanks to a mixture of heavyweight snaring and poisoning, said Graham. 'If it's done well enough over a large enough area it probably does have an effect.'

'In some situations fox control just prior to the birds' breeding season gives birds a window of opportunity, so productivity does increase,' said Graham. They were clear that the RSPB wasn't trying to control foxes in terms of populations, just in order to create a time window for the priority bird species to breed successfully.

The control measures the RSPB do take are careful and as humane as possible. They talked of their love of foxes; certain reserves encourage people to look out for them.

Fox control is a highly controversial topic, and the way forward is not clear – there are many different motivations, methods and conflicting studies muddying the waters. It does make sense, however, to remember that human behaviour plays a significant part. The 'problem' of the fox is exacerbated by the same thing that helps 10,000 species to go extinct each year and the polar ice caps to melt: our treatment of the earth and its resources. Without the endangered curlew, hedgehog or metallic tansy beetle, our lives will be much poorer and thinner. Without the fox, they would be, too. For the moment, killing foxes is still perfectly legal. There is, however, one method that has been banned, and that is where the debate around foxes rages most bitterly: hunting with dogs.

4

Tally Ho!

Hunting has long been a pursuit of passion in Britain. George Osbaldeston (1786–1866), known as the 'Squire of England', was a celebrity during the 'Golden Age of Hunting'. He drew hushed glances from followers when he arrived at a meet, for stories of his sporting prowess, such as the day he'd supposedly killed 98 pheasants with 100 shots, were often the talk of the hunting world. The Squire's hounds, which he bred himself, were said at one time to have the best blood in Britain.

It was a biting day to be outside. The ash, hazel and sycamore trees were starting to bud and the bushes had been filled with the song of reed buntings and sedge warblers the previous week, but the wind was high and specks of snow drove into the faces of the hunters. Squire George was a little hung-over and tired from his social activities. He'd played whist and billiards with friends for fifty-five hours straight in a bid to recoup some of the £200,000 he'd recently lost gambling recklessly at the races. The strong ale from the night before had gone to his head but, nevertheless, he'd turned up at the Heythrop Hunt looking as smart

as ever, in his red coat, breeches and top hat, all made by
the finest tailors in Mayfair.

George was not a tall man, but at 5 foot 6 and weighing
around 11 stone, he had the perfect physique to rocket over
hedges and fences. Someone once described him as having
the features of a fox cub, and he was good-looking, with large,
dark eyes, a fine crop of hair and cheeks often flushed crimson. With the wind on his face, blowing his horn and riding
his favourite hunting horse, Assheton, he was in his element.
Even though the hunt had been riding for hours with no luck
(they'd covered over 27 kilometres of Oxfordshire country –
foxes these days were scarce), he was in high spirits.

Suddenly, the pace of the hunt accelerated. A fox had
flown across the flat, dry grassland out of a covert. George
couldn't keep his horse from riding full pelt to the hounds.
Standing in his stirrups, mesmerised by the pack following the orange comet, he was in a reverie. Then, his horse
caught its hoof in a drain and George tumbled off, falling
smack on his back on the stone path. The last things he saw
were the eyes and teeth of his friend Sir James Musgrave's
horse as it trampled him. When George came round he saw
bone protruding from his broken leg and his boot overflow-
ing with blood. At one point it seemed the leg would have to
be amputated; although it was saved in the end, for a while
he considered giving up his favourite sport. That didn't last,
though. He soon went back to hunting his own hounds – his

'dear children' – six days a week and the legend continued. His kind of passion and commitment to the sport is still seen across Britain to this day.

In some ways, modern hunts, in lands ribboned with motorways and railway lines, are different from the vast, epic traditional hunts of the mid-nineteenth century that would cover miles and last for hours. These days, hunts might take about two hours, or less, depending on the fox's health and stamina, the weather and the conditions for catching a scent. Of course, hunting and killing the fox has been banned in England and Wales since the Hunting Act of 2004 (Scotland brought a ban in a couple of years earlier, in 2002), amid plenty of controversy. But the tradition of the hunt itself continues and many of the essential practices remain the same today as they did during the Golden Age. Some say people still hunt foxes with the same gusto, as if it had never been banned, unbeknown to much of the general public. After all, 50,000 hunters signed the 'Hunting Declaration', which pledged that, if a law was passed, they would disobey it and continue to hunt. It is my impression, from various conversations, that some hunts are participating in legal hunting, but in all likelihood there are others that ignore the Act – a law they utterly abhor – and continue chasing foxes as they always have. Unless observed by monitors, it is an easy activity to get away with, because hunting takes place on private land.

Traditional fox hunting takes place at around eleven o'clock in the morning on Saturdays, and sometimes on two other mornings a week, depending on the area. The hunt and its followers will gather at the 'meet', which is normally held at someone's house, a local landmark, on the village green or in front of a pub. The group will chat and socialise; non-subscribers pay their 'cap', a fee for a day out hunting, to the secretary. Port or whisky may be drunk and possibly a bacon sandwich or other such nibbles will be on offer.

Preparation for the hunt will have started hours in advance. Before dawn, the grooms will have fed and prepared the horses, and the huntsman will have readied the hounds at the kennel. Many of the participants will have been up early as well, ironing their garments in order to look sharp as a nail. Taking pride in appearance is a tradition of hunting, and many will take a long time to get ready.

Different hunts have different sartorial rules, although all ask that people turn up looking neat, clean and tidy with a groomed horse and polished tack. Some will wear the traditional scarlet coats, or 'pink' as it is known, named after Thomas Pink, the eighteenth-century tailor who designed them; others will wear tweed, ratcatchers or black coats. The red coats are a sign of status and, alongside the prestigious 'hunt button', a brass badge with the hunt's distinctive monogram, initials and often a running fox, are usually worn by those with a number of years' experience. Hunt staff will also often wear the red coats to make them easy to identify. In recent years, though, the red coats have become less popular, presumably because the bright colour draws unwanted attention. In the past, a top hat and tails were worn for certain hunts as well, though these were generally phased out in the early nineteenth century in favour of hats that would stay on the head during bumpy rides or while riding under low-hanging tree branches. The website of the New Forest Hounds, however, still mentions the option of a top hat. The accessories are important, too: proper waterproof riding boots, spurs worn high along the ankle seam of the boot and a hunting tie secured with a long, gold-coloured pin.

Similarly, etiquette and good manners are vital components. There are strict rules about behaving responsibly on the 'country', the area of land made available by the landowner. Partly, this is because the hunt is at the liberty of the farmer or other landowner who has given permission for scores of people to ride over his land. Speaking politely, saying 'gate please' when walking through an open gate, and obeying orders are crucial to the smooth running of the day.

Once assembled, the hunt will move off, led by the Master, who is the person in charge. He or she will also decide which coverts are to be 'drawn', meaning which wooded areas to send the hounds into to find a fox. Later, he or she will decide when the hunt is over. Sometimes, there are a few Joint Masters. Hunt followers are required to say 'Good morning, Master' when they arrive, and 'Goodbye and thank you, Master' when they leave. The Huntsman's job is to control the hounds with his horn, making sure they're obedient and behaving correctly. The Whipper-In is a hunt staff member who assists the Huntsman – the name carried through to the 'whip' and 'chief whip' of politics.

The group on horseback following the hounds is called the Field. They 'ride the hounds' and are looked after by the Fieldmaster, who makes sure they're not too close to distract or hinder the work of the pack, and are riding responsibly. Behind the mounted Field will be 'foot followers' who are, confusingly, following in their cars. Of course, this is a relatively new part of the culture of hunting. They will follow the group as much as they can on country roads, using binoculars and staying dry. Some hunts will have actual foot followers, and fell packs, those in hilly areas, are all on foot.

Once the hunt moves off, the group follows the hounds, who, before the ban and possibly still nowadays, would be looking for a 'line' or trail of fox odour. A hound is said to 'open' when he catches the scent from the fox's foot glands. It depends on the ground and soil, but, in general, scent is harder to catch for the hounds on dry, hot days because the scent molecules will evaporate quickly, and on windy days, as they will be dispersed. A cold, dry day apparently gives the ideal scenting conditions. The hound 'gives tongue' or 'speaks' – basically howls – once the scent is caught. Sometimes the hounds will 'check', which means they have lost the scent. Often the scent will be caught in a covert, or a patch of wood, and the hounds will be called out with a horn if the fox breaks cover. Then the hunt really begins, with the hounds whizzing after 'Charlie', and everyone else dashing after the hounds at various distances. A hound is a good dog if it has 'drive', which means it is yearning to catch the 'line' and get the fox. If they succeed, the hounds will kill the fox by ripping it apart.

Sometimes, the fox will escape into a hole in the ground for protection. It might be its own home, or den, or a lucky find along the way. This is when the terriers come in. Terriermen are another group in the hunt. They follow, often on a quad-bike, with specially trained dogs, smaller than the hounds, who can fit into the underground holes and dig out the fox. A terrierman will then shoot the fox, although occasionally the terrier might have already killed it.

Most people on the hunt won't actually see the kill of the fox; however a successful day out hunting ends with the death of 'Charlie'.

A traditional fox-hunting custom is 'blooding', when the blood of the fox is smeared on the cheeks of a new member of the hunt. The ritual was introduced by King James I in the seventeenth century and is also used as an initiation ritual in other field sports such as pheasant-shooting. The blood daubed must be of the first fox the child or novice has seen being killed as a sort of rural baptism. It is difficult to tell how often the tradition takes place today as it is a ritual that incites criticism from anti-hunting activists so is not one to shout about.

As we've seen, fox hunting has been a tradition in Britain as far back as the tenth century, evolving through the millennia until its fairly recent ban. The change in attitudes to animal welfare and animal-related sports had started in the eighteenth century, but in the case of fox hunting, it really picked up pace only during the twentieth century. So how did the ban come into effect?

One reason is that people have increasingly been moving away from the countryside – by 2050, it is thought that 89 per cent of the population in Britain will live in urban areas. The children and grandchildren of people who hunt – whether they be farmers or farmhands, huntsmen or ironmongers, terriermen or landed gentry – are no longer in the countryside to uphold the traditions. That is not to say people don't still hunt – plenty do, and many of the big, fashionable hunts are now supported by wealthy London residents – but the migration to urban areas has contributed, among other things, to the change in attitudes to hunting. Gradually, fox hunting became less fashionable and concern over the ethics of the practice became more widespread.

The main point for debate was the suffering of the fox, both during the pursuit and in the manner of its death. The arguments over whether the fox suffers through hunting are complicated. Pro-hunting groups say that it doesn't, that it's actually the most humane form of control and a much more natural way for the fox to die than poisoning or shooting. There's even an argument that the fox enjoys the hunt. There was a strong sense in the hunting literature I read that 'Charlie' can experience 'fun'. The fox was often depicted as having a whale of a time during the hunt, tricking his opponents, running across bridges and walls, looking back at the hunters chasing him with a gleeful smile and a lick of the lips.

Wildlife photographer Richard Bowler, whose foxes have granted him an opportunity to see fox behaviour up close, had a different take on that 'smile': 'When Rosie comes up to see me she's almost smiling,' he said. 'When other foxes are nearby she's also almost smiling with her tongue out, but it's stress. Even with Hetty, she'll come out, she's got this grin, she won't settle, she's getting a stress look. It looks like she's really grinning.'

I asked a Master of Foxhounds, Andrew Cook, if he'd seen signs of stress in the fox running away from the hounds. 'I'd be lying if I said I'd not,' he said, 'but 95 per cent of the time I'd say when a fox is hunted, it's not been stressed. I don't think a fox thinks until the last few seconds that it's in too much danger.'

Another high-profile fox hunter I spoke to, the philosopher Roger Scruton, argued similarly. 'As anyone who witnessed the death knows, it's instantaneous because it's a tiny thing suddenly jumped on by huge creatures which just tear it apart in an instant. It's kinder than the death of a mouse in the jaws of a cat. It's not the death that is particularly disturbing. Of course if the thing is frightened hour after hour . . . but on the whole the hunts only last for twenty minutes. Very rarely is it killed; it's usually got away by then.'

Opponents of hunting would argue that the fox rarely takes a couple of seconds to be killed and, alongside the prolonged chase causing suffering, that this is not a humane way to die.

A report for the National Trust in 1997, conducted by Cambridge Professor Patrick Bateson, showed that deer are not adapted to being hunted with hounds. High concentrations of cortisol were found in blood and muscle samples of sixty-four hunted deer: levels typically associated with high levels of physiological and psychological stress. A similar study does not exist for the fox, but the supposition from animal welfare groups is that it is similarly harmful. However, different scientists interpret data in different ways, and both sides have rubbished each other's methods at one time or another. Unfortunately, we cannot ask a fox whether it hurts to be hunted.

Although there is no consensus on the most humane way to kill a fox, it is possible that alternative ways could be as inhumane as hunting – a farmer who's a bad shot, for example – but the different sides disagree on wounding rates. The tentative conclusion of the Burns Inquiry, the government committee set up in 1999 specifically to look at the facts of the debate, was that lamping using rifles, if carried out properly and in appropriate circumstances, had fewer adverse welfare implications than hunting, including digging out. It stated that the experience of being closely pursued, caught and killed above ground by hounds, 'seriously compromises the welfare of the fox'. Although there is no firm scientific evidence, the inquiry was satisfied that the activity of digging out and shooting a fox also involves a serious compromise of its welfare, bearing in mind the often protracted nature of the process and the fact that the fox is prevented from escaping.

On the wave of this debate, Tony Blair, then prime minister and leader of the Labour Party, promised to ban fox hunting in 1999. In 2000, five options were presented: allow hunting to continue in its present form; implement a total ban; introduce a limited ban; licensed hunting; or address the matter with local referendums. Sports Minister Kate Hoey formed the Middle Way Group, intended to prevent a wholesale ban, calling for licences for hunting with hounds and a national team of inspectors. 'We found a middle way about Sunday shopping. Perhaps we will find a middle way about this,' said Liberal Democrat MP Lembit Opik at the time.

In 2001, MPs backed the total ban on fox hunting (387 to 174), while also rejecting proposals for self-regulation (399 to 155) and licensed hunting (382 to 182). It was argued that licences didn't address the cruelty of the chase. The response to the announcement saw a surge in opposition from the pro-hunt community with over 400,000 marching through London in September 2002 to show their support for fox hunting.

MPs backed the ban again but the House of Lords voted for hunting to continue, which resulted in parliamentary clashes and attempts at a compromise for years. Eventually the Lords were ignored and the Parliament Act invoked. The Countryside Alliance attempted to obstruct the bill one last time, at the court of appeal, suggesting that the use of the Parliament Act nullified the ban. The court of appeal, however, upheld its previous ruling; with all obstructions finally removed, the ban came into effect on Friday, 18 February 2005.

The pro-hunt side argued that the Act was passed by people who didn't understand how hunting works, and why it was needed. It believed that Labour supporters thought of hunting as a 'posh' activity, and some MPs and many on the pro-hunting side saw banning it as part of a 'class war'. It was also thought that some politicians were using it to score political points, that a hunting ban would get more support for their political party.

However, the general public did seem to be on the side of those politicians. A MORI poll in 1997 found that 71 per cent of the UK population agreed that hunting with hounds should be banned; 72 per cent disagreed that hunting was necessary to control fox numbers; and 66 per cent disagreed that hunting with hounds was an important part of the rural economy. In March 2002, another MORI poll showed that 72 per cent of the public thought that fox hunting should be illegal (the figures were 80 per cent for deer hunting and 81 per cent for hare coursing). Ten years after the ban, in 2015, an Ipsos MORI poll found that a majority of the British public was still in favour of many of the bans included in the Hunting Act: fox hunting (83 per cent); deer hunting (85 per cent); hare hunting and coursing (87 per cent); dog fighting (98 per cent); and badger baiting (94 per cent). The final study had a sample size of 2,000, the others of 1,000.

It does depend who you ask. A poll in the same year on the *Telegraph* website, a pro-hunting newspaper with a strong rural readership, found that 43 per cent of people supported a repeal of the fox-hunting ban; another, commissioned by the Countryside Alliance, the leading campaign group for the sport, found that only 40 per cent believed it should be a criminal offence. These are outliers, though; the majority of polls suggest the public is in favour of the ban, although the hunting side would question the right of the public, who mostly live in urban areas, to impose their views and rule over the rural minority.

For most people who don't have the time or access to commission their own personal studies of heart rates and hormone levels – and, indeed, consider that 700 hours of parliamentary debate failed to provide a scientific consensus – a decision on harm and suffering will be made on a basic, emotional level: it is difficult for a mammal not to assume that being chased by dogs and ripped apart is a negative experience, whether the pro-hunting groups say it's kind or not.

In a celebrity-focused world, the words of an animal-loving famous person can have significant influence. Within wider environmental issues, it is also much easier to mobilise fans to care about cute dolphins, lions or cuddly fox cubs, rather than the slightly more abstract threat of climate change. The comedian Ricky Gervais is one of the most outspoken opponents of cruelty against animals. Big game and fox hunting are his main targets. He talks to his nearly 11 million Twitter followers as much about animal welfare as he does about his work. Among the tweets about *Derek*, *Special Correspondents* or *The Office*, his stream is filled with calls to donate to charities that campaign against experimentation on animals and to sign petitions to ban the Chinese Yulin

Dog Meat Festival, as well as pictures of his cats. He regularly thanks his fans for putting up with his animal welfare updates, which he describes as the more 'serious business', compared with promoting his new show or film.

I was in Toronto, Canada, to interview Gervais on the set of his latest film for a London-based magazine. Occasionally, a small group of journalists has to interview a subject in a round-table session. I was hoping this wouldn't be the case, so I could ask Gervais about vulpine matters. On arrival, I discovered that I'd be interviewing with two other journalists in the room. We would share questions over a twenty-minute period. Every question had to count. I mentioned it to the others knowing full well that it would be pretty annoying to have time taken up with something completely unrelated to our briefs. They sweetly said it was fine so, at the eleventh hour, I took the plunge. Gervais had been charming, witty, generous and easy throughout the day. I asked him a simple question – Following the recent effort to repeal the hunting ban, why were foxes so loved and hated in Britain? – and it opened the floodgates. The monologue crescendoed as Gervais became more and more – knowingly, laughingly, amusingly – irate.

'I don't think they are hated and treated so badly in Britain,' he began. 'It's a privileged few who do it. Think how many people actually go fox hunting out of 60 million people. It's ludicrous. We've got the most powerful man in

Britain in charge doing this because he likes it and his mates like it. What good is it for? It's ludicrous. Every argument you see for fox hunting is false, OK? They wouldn't like it if it's a robot fox. They like hunting the fox and seeing it.

'What's all the bloody stuff for?' he said, referring to the practice when young hunters are blooded for the first time. 'What's all that for? It's sick. It's something twisted. If it really is a cull, let's do it humanely. They say, "Oh, it is humane." Oh, is that why Dignitas rip apart old people with foxes [dogs] when they want to die? No, it's not humane. Anything that's gratuitous or done for the spectacle and the sport is wrong. If that fox really had to die . . . I had to put my cat down, I cried my eyes out and at no point did the vet go, "Do you mind if I send my dogs on it for a laugh and take a selfie?" It's because they like it and enjoy it and it's for a privileged few. Don't give me this "it's tradition". So was slavery. They say that about fucking bullfighting. It's disgusting. Who wants to see a bull tortured to death for an hour? I did a tweet once, someone had said, "It's an effective form of pest control." I said, "The only way it's an effective form of pest control is if the posh twats fell off their horse and broke their necks."'

He paused for breath and I looked at my fellow journalists apologetically.

Although fox hunting is now ostensibly banned, there are still 186 packs of foxhounds in England, Scotland and Wales. So, what are they doing? Officially, drag or trail hunting. Drag hunting is a sport that dates back to the 1800s and involves placing down a scent in a known spot on a predetermined route for bloodhounds and foxhounds to follow. Most of the scents used incorporate human or animal urine mixed with aniseed, chemicals, water and oil. However, it is not always a fox-based scent; sometimes the bloodhound pack will chase the scent of a human runner – which, considering it is a fast-paced sport that involves lots of jumping, sounds terrifying.

Trail hunting is slightly different. It was invented when the Hunting Act was passed in 2004. Unlike drag hunting, the trail will be unknown to the Field, so it's more exciting and unpredictable. It also involves the hunting of a scent laid by humans, but it's supposed to simulate traditional hunting activity with the scent mimicking the fox and dabbed through various coverts and countryside areas. Trail hunting is not welcomed by hunters. The Countryside Alliance describes it as an 'interim measure forced upon us by the Hunting Act that is necessary to maintain the infrastructure of hunting'. It is seen as a necessary measure while the 'temporary' ban is enforced to keep the hounds exercised. The Alliance, in its Hunting Handbook, is adamant that the scent should always be fox-based so that the hounds remain focused on its scent for the eventual return of hunting. One supplier of fox urine for hunts and the Countryside Alliance is Adrian's Fox Scent. The website sells 100-millilitre bottles for £35, which seems like quite a lot for fox piss.

'For people who want to gallop around on horses, it's fine,' explained Andrew Cook about drag and trail hunting. 'But for the purist, the venery side is not comparable at all.'

One of the reasons anti-hunting groups oppose trail hunting is because it still teaches the pack how to smell for and catch a fox. If the hounds are still trained to follow the scent of a fox, what's going to stop them attacking if they come across one? If the hounds do find a fox, and it's spotted by one of the hunters, who'll usually cry out 'Tally Ho' according to tradition, they are supposed to pull the hounds away from the fox.

Although many hunts claim that's what they do, the League Against Cruel Sports, the Hunt Saboteurs Association, the International Fund for Animal Welfare and others maintain that hunting is happening as it always has. The League is supportive of drag hunting – using a non-fox-based scent – but believes trail hunting is a cover for illegal hunting. A look at forums and accounts on various hunting websites and social media, as well as the evidence collected by hunt monitors, suggests that, in some areas, the League is right.

The risk of a conviction (the penalty is a fine of up to £5,000, which anti-hunting campaigners such as the League argue is much too low; they want to introduce a six-month prison sentence) and the passion and anger around which hunters have fought to keep their sport suggest there must be a profound benefit to those who do it. So, why do people hunt?

I have some insight into this, as members of my family in Scotland have been keen hunters. These days, like many families, the younger generation has mostly moved away from the countryside and into the cities. I was never around long enough to go hunting and it didn't really appeal. I was far from a natural at riding a horse, which I found a bit frightening, and things like music and pubs were more interesting to me as a teenager. Later, no one I knew did it, so it rarely came up, and I couldn't get my head around the final act. But my grandfather, with whom I was very close, was passionate about hunting.

As a child, I was lucky to spend lots of hours outdoors in Galloway, Scotland, when visiting my grandparents' rather remote house on the coast. It was a place of trees and soil, night skies mad with stars, dogs and tobogganing and butterflies and tree-houses and toffee. I can easily summon the creak of wooden stairs as we ran down to breakfast before heading outside to the woods, moors or coastland. It was a blissful place to spend holidays and I cried to leave. My late grandfather farmed but also left much of his land to grow wild and thick. Looking across to the Lake District from the hills he managed, bruised purple with heather, a buzzard flying ahead, it's still my favourite place in the world. When I swim in the sea, or ramble through the forests, it's the place that makes me feel most alive.

Although I never saw my grandfather in his white britches, red coat and riding hat – he stopped hunting before I was born – hunting was a strong presence at his house. Portraits of horses and hounds were dotted around the rooms that stood next to stables and outhouses where the real horses and hounds lived. Fox heads – 'masks' as they're called – hung on the walls of the first room by the front door alongside models of Spitfires suspended from the ceiling and bookshelves filled with hunting literature.

My grandfather was brought up in a strict, Quaker-like, church-going household. His father, a tobacco businessman, felt that his eight children needed a hobby instead of going to dances or music-halls so he bought them ponies and dogs, which sparked my grandfather's love of animals. His older brother started farming in Northumberland and, in the school holidays, he'd go up to the farm to ride. This was the mid-1930s, before the war, while he was at school in London. He quickly became hooked on the outdoors and riding. Soon, whenever he visited his brother, he'd get up early to trot 25 kilometres to join others at the local hunt meet and ride off into deeper countryside. Everything changed when he was nineteen. The Second World War broke out and he spent the next few years, between the ages of twenty and twenty-six, in the army. His experience of war ended with witnessing first hand the atrocities of the Nazi concentration camp of Bergen-Belsen.

He returned from the war keen to ride and hunt again, physically affected by sleeping in or under tanks for much of his twenties, and, I imagine, traumatised. He moved between farms in Scotland, Sussex and Northumberland, and eventually settled in Galloway. He started breeding foxhounds, imported hares to the area – to look at – and campaigned for the rights of maltreated local timber ponies in the woods of Dumfriesshire. In the early 1960s, he investigated cases of misuse and poor welfare and suggested that a safeguard for the ponies' care should be written into contracts. He worked with the RSPCA, and the matter was brought to national level and carried through.

While he was alive, I understood that my grandfather loved hunting, and later I was told by my grandmother that it was details like the noses of the hounds as they got the scent, the horses and being out in the countryside that motivated him to hunt. He loved the writings of Sassoon and Trollope. Sassoon's *Memoirs of a Fox-Hunting Man* would have had a particular resonance, as it centres on the life of a man who discovers hunting before enlisting to fight in the war. My grandfather had a similar experience, falling for riding and hunting before the war, and getting back into them again afterwards.

After the trauma of war, riding was an activity that soothed and helped him recover. Hunting provided exercise and healing for his body, and fresh air. I imagine it was an escape for him, to watch the hounds and ride his horse – and he rode every single day until he was unable to do so. After that, he'd watch films of hunting at home.

Next to the television in the study, there is a painting on the wall. It's a military lithograph by the wartime artist 'Snaffles' (Charles Johnson Payne) depicting a scene from the First World War. Two men sit in the trenches, wet, cold, scared. They are smoking pipes, just as my grandfather used to. In the image, one man is on lookout, standing and peering into the distance with a gun. Swirling around the soldiers is a dream sequence of a hunt: the hounds, a man in a red coat on a horse. The men are dreaming of their days out in the countryside on horseback, the smell of spring, sun on their backs and fresh air in their lungs. As in many paintings of fox hunting, the fox is absent – the focus is on the tradition and experience of the hunt itself.

If you'd seen death on the level those soldiers did, the occasional demise of a fox at the expense of profound human pleasure, so needed after a war, might be less complicated, especially if you believed foxes needed to be killed anyway and death by hounds was the kindest way.

I wondered, too, if soldiers returning from war were so used to a high level of adrenal intensity that they 'fed' it through the sport of fox hunting, which could be extremely dangerous, exciting and adrenaline-producing in itself. There might be a link between the adrenaline of war and the continuation of hunting. Sufferers of post-traumatic stress disorder referred to it as an 'addiction to adrenaline'. The men coming back from the war might have needed hunting in a way that I could never truly understand.

To try to understand more about the desire to hunt, I turned to my grandfather's bookshelves and his collection of old hunting texts. I quickly found a passage in Frederick Watson's *Hunting Pie* which runs through lots of reasons why hunting happens, with tongue firmly in cheek, including 'for the socialists, Communists, Pacifists, and other vegetarians prepared to perish in Bermondsey for Russia, who would be gravely rationed in rhetoric without the red-coated tyrants of old England', suggesting that, without hunting, the left-wingers would have nothing to complain about. 'Despite railways, tarmac, wire, taxation, motors, financial depression and the falsetto outcries of professional humanitarians,' he writes, hunting still continues. 'Now you are satisfied that it exists purely and completely to serve the good offices of industry, economics, democracy. Or aren't you? Personally I am not. I believe, and will continue to believe, that people, whether they are PMs or prime simpletons or whether they lived in the eighteenth or twentieth centuries, galloped after foxes for one reason only. What, pray, was that? Because it's such jolly good fun.'

The first, most obvious reason why people enjoy hunting must be this: that riding around the beautiful British countryside is, quite simply, a lark. Forget the fact of the death of a fox for now (for most won't see that and some can easily put it out of their mind). It is not controversial to assert that exercise and being outside in the fresh air are good for a person.

For some, the joys to be found in fox hunting are incomparable. Roger Scruton sets out why he fell completely head over heels in love with the sport in his 1998 book *On Hunting*, in which he divides his life into three parts: 'In the first, I was wretched; in the second, ill at ease; in the third, hunting.'

He compared the collective activity of hunting to football obsession or supporting a sports team. There is a sense that hunting for Roger was as much about life as it was about death. The 'seventeen-hand horses were snorting and heaving to every side, their buttocks rippling with muscle like the seething wakes of ocean liners', he wrote, electrified by the movement of animals around him. Hunting was 'the very dance of death and regeneration which was skirting the wet ditches of this blighted farm-land and bringing it against the odds to life'.

In another passage from the book, he continues to describe that vitality: 'The blood of another species flows through your veins, stirring the old deposits, of collective life, releasing pockets of energy that a million generations laboriously harvested from the crop of human suffering.'

He also emphasised the importance of the relationship between man and hound, man and horse, horse and hound. His horse, Dumbo, changed completely when hunting; he 'suffered a metamorphosis as far-fetched as any in Ovid, he had rediscovered his life'.

Like Plato, who wrote that hunting was a noble activity that teaches young people knowledge, problem-solving and how to get around and be part of the countryside, Roger believes it is also character-building. 'The courage part is still there,' he told me. 'If you're riding a horse across country it's quite a dangerous thing that requires personal courage. Then of course, there is discipline,' he continued. 'The fact that you are, like in an army, reduced to the condition of someone who takes orders.'

In fact, hunting has traditionally been a highly valued part of British military life – particularly for the officer corps of the late nineteenth century – seen to inspire efficiency and discipline. It was also a way of practising certain military skills, not just horse riding, but learning to analyse and quickly traverse unfamiliar landscapes, so it was an important part of training for colonial warfare.

As the cavalry was mostly made up of upper-class men with private incomes, educated at public schools, the majority would already have been familiar with hunting, and it was made readily available to them in the military. Percival Marling, a recipient of the Victoria Cross, wrote that in Tipperary in the 1880s, hunting was available six days a week; the same was true in Aldershot, where leave was also granted without question for hunting and regiments would often keep a pack of hounds.

Hunting continued to be an essential component of training into the twentieth century with the outbreak of the First World War – some packs of hounds even joined regiments at the front. In the 1930s, the 6th Royal Inniskilling Dragoon Guards would go away each winter to hunt for two months.

The importance of hunting diminished as advances in technology, such as tanks, started to replace cavalry units, and the lavish culture of the officer class was gradually dismantled. By 1952, the change had become apparent, as Winston Churchill ruled that officers keen to hunt foxes in Lower Saxony (part of occupied Germany after the Second World War, where fox hunting was banned) must respect the desires of the inhabitants. 'The prime minister has expressed the following view: "Do the Germans really object to fox hunting by British troops in Lower Saxony? If they do, it should be stopped. You may occupy a country, but that does not give you unlimited freedom to indulge in sports which annoy the inhabitants,"' wrote Churchill's private secretary, Anthony Montague Browne, to the War Office.

The decree was not well received by those who still wished to enjoy their sporting pursuit: 'The action proposed by the Germans in this respect is somewhat the same as if we were to introduce a law in the UK making baseball illegal for the American Air Forces,' grumbled the British commander Sir John Harding.

Related to the enjoyment of a hunt is a social element, which is particularly important for those living in rural areas. The Burns Inquiry committee travelled the country talking to people about hunting when working out whether it should be banned. They found that the loss of hunting would be keenly felt in isolated rural communities. Those who would not feel greatly, at a personal level, the loss of the hunts' social activities still believed it would have a detrimental effect on the social life of others and on community life in general. 'Hunting acts as a significant cohesive force, encouraging a system of mutual support,' the committee wrote. They also concluded that farmers, as a group, felt that their interests and way of life were not understood by Westminster and the urban majority. Fox hunting has fuelled the perceived divide between town- and country-dwellers for decades.

On the other hand, it might be said to have brought

the countryside together. Roger Scruton explains: 'It subsidises not only the hounds, huntsmen and kennel, it returns money to farmers in one way or another; the hunt is always organising things.' The hunt will often remove fallen stock such as dead cows and dispose of them as a favour to the farmer, who would normally have to pay £200. Roger also emphasised the inclusion of farmers, housewives and children, which allows the various classes to get to know each other and depend on each other. 'It breaks down social barriers in a hugely creative way,' he said.

A farmer with a particular problem fox will also call the local hunt and ask them to come and kill it. 'What hunts should be very good at is responding to farmers' requests,' said veteran fox hunter Brian Fanshawe. 'If the farmer has got a particular problem with a fox taking poultry, piglets or lambs, there are calls and they go early in the morning for the hounds to get the scent of the fox.' This particularly happens in upland areas, where it is easier to hunt foxes than control them through lamping and shooting because of the terrain.

Tradition plays an important part as well. The majority of people who go fox hunting have grown up in families that hunt. And for those who move to the countryside, their children might develop an interest in hunting because it gives much greater access to the countryside, instead of just boring bridleways. If your child wants to ride a pony at the weekend, it will be allowed only on public footpaths.

Many counties – Hampshire is one – are made up of plenty of privately owned land. To ride freely across the most beautiful parts of the countryside, having a relationship with the local farmers and landowners, helps immensely. If they already allow the hunt to use their land, the opportunity already exists – if, that is, the child's parents are supportive of the act of hunting itself.

The hunt is also a ceremony of great theatre and performance, and the need for rituals is a basic instinct. Humans are highly social animals and we bond in groups, communities, and as a society, through shared events and habitual practices. To connect regularly, to share in a uniform, language, social circle and, in the case of hunting, common passion, boosts personal identity – and psychologists have shown that traditions and rituals can have an important psychological impact on emotions and behaviour. When the law was passed and the rural minority faced not being able to hunt, it wasn't just killing foxes that was threatened, it was the whole complex pattern of social interactions, shared experiences and a powerful sense of unity and comradeship. Hunting is, on this level, a simple bonding experience. Returning to my grandfather's library, I found a strong sense of identity and loyalty among the hunters. Being a 'fox-hunting man' meant you were a jolly good sort.

It's an emotional experience, too: the visceral excitement of the hunt, its performance and pageantry, and the rich soundscape from the chorus of hounds. The countryside was designed for hunting, after all, and it must be pretty exciting to hightail it around on the back of a galloping horse, jumping over hedgerows and fences. The anthropologist Garry Marvin has spent years with different hunts, and has written comprehensive, lucid and fascinating essays on the subject, explaining the 'fusion and completeness' of the humans, hounds and fox as being 'totally engaged with each other; a web of lines, flows and intensities being pulled tight'.

As he puts it: 'As the hounds close in on the fox with the riders behind them, an emotional connection with the countryside has been fully realised. This is marked by total involvement, a total immersion, in the event by all the participants. So intense is this moment of the full occurrence of hunting that there is no space for reflection or thought – instincts and passions flow together. It is a moment beyond meaning. What has been imagined, desired, and worked for comes together with full absorption into the activity. This crescendo of excitement and intensity is halted abruptly. The fox is killed and all activity, except for the pack surging around the dead body, ceases. The Huntsman blows the haunting call of "the kill" and this hunt event is finished. But, to return to an initial point of this piece, this death is merely the appropriate way of bringing the performance to a conclusion.'

The Countryside Alliance however, plays down the

recreational elements, and focuses on wildlife management and pest control. In a pamphlet called 'An introduction to fox hunting', the reasons given for hunting include: 'to protect other species that are vulnerable to predation; to prevent over population because when there are too many of any one species food and habitat can run short; to protect farm livestock by dispersing and reducing high populations of predators; to protect against the spread of diseases which can break out when there are too many of any one species; and because we have a duty of care for the welfare of wild animals'. It differentiates wildlife management from pest control by stating that while management aims to keep a population healthy and at an acceptable level, pest control seeks to eradicate a population, regardless of whether individuals are sick, old or indeed healthy.

Charlie Pye-Smith, a writer on rural sports and hunting, wrote in his book *Rural Rites* that hunting 'aims to keep populations of wild mammals below the level where they would be regarded as pests, and possibly subject to more brutal methods of control'. He makes the case that the hunt is, paradoxically, one of the fox's most powerful allies. In *The Facts of Rural Life*, he argues in favour of wildlife management, writing of the 'scientific rationale for controlling species whose populations have risen following the loss of apex predators'. The most controversial topic in conservation ecology – the role of predation and how predators should be managed in wildlife ecosystems – is inseparable from the topic of hunting. Often welfarists and conservationists even within 'Team Fox' will disagree.

However, the League and other anti-hunting groups would say that there is evidence that hunts actually preserve foxes, which would put an end to any arguments of wildlife management or pest control. They cite instances where video footage has been taken of hunt terriermen allegedly dumping tubs of offal on land for foxes to eat, preserving den sites and artificial earths. In June 2015, sixteen fox cubs were found in a barn in North Yorkshire. DNA testing found that they were from four separate litters, which suggests this wasn't just a very large litter coincidentally near to hunt kennels. If these cubs were being raised to be killed for sport, it significantly threatens the wildlife management claim – and would be a criminal offence.

The argument for population control is also undermined by statistics, in that hunting never accounted for the majority of animals killed. The GWCT study, mentioned in Chapter 3, found that, before the ban, hunting with dogs as a method of culling foxes was widespread in the three regions surveyed. The proportion of farmers who actively participated was between 35 and 54 per cent, although the intensity of hunt culling varied between the regions. However, the study also found that farmers significantly overestimated the number of foxes culled by the hunts and gun packs in all three regions. Overall, when hunting was legal, on top of the estimated 80,000 foxes shot by farmers and gamekeepers each year, only a further 16,000 to 21,000 foxes were killed on the hunts.

The Countryside Alliance also believes that 'wild mammals do not feel fear in the same way humans do. Hunting is totally natural to them' and that 'there has never been any evidence that hunting is less humane than other ways of killing foxes'.

This argument about hunting being natural in the animal world could potentially have merit. It is true that humans were hunter-gatherers in the past. There is a theory that meat-eating helped humans evolve larger brains with high-energy food supporting brain development so, in a way, hunting helped us evolve into the species we are today. Roger Scruton believes there's something in human nature that finds gratification in hunting. 'You are returning to something deep in yourself,' he said. 'However, it doesn't follow that that's a good thing because there's lots of things deep in us that we want to get away from, in particular the tendency to murder rival tribes.'

Hunting might also fulfil a need that's been lost over the years: the achievement of gathering food. 'It might be that that hunt, that chase, that kill is something that we've lost as a society because we're so dissociated with our food,' said Dawn Scott.

Perhaps if the fox was eaten at the end of the hunt, the process would be much more palatable for a greater number of people. It is the pursuit of an inedible animal – as Oscar Wilde put it, 'the unspeakable in pursuit of the inedible' – that makes the practice an invented cultural pursuit, and not a natural one in the way, for example, hunting deer or boar for dinner would be.

One thing that is hard for many of the anti-fox-hunting supporters to understand is that people who participate in the hunt don't necessarily hate foxes: many tend to respect them, and some even love them.

The fox certainly wasn't a hated animal at my grandparents' house. It was respected and admired. My first experience of the fox was a cuddly puppet, 'Foxy'. It was a small toy with red-orange fur and plastic eyes, and it sat on the top of a bookshelf in the study, looking across to the Solway Firth. My grandfather was a master storyteller and joker. He played games with his young grandchildren – Up Jenkins was a favourite – and had a strong streak of mischief. He was quick to pull funny faces to make us laugh. 'Foxy's gonna get you' was a game he played with the puppet when we were children. He'd come and say goodnight to us, tuck us up in bed and put the fox under the sheets as if it was chasing us. We remember it fondly.

And I found plenty of examples of other pro-hunting people only too ready to share their love of foxes. Brian Fanshawe's early experience of hunting was helping his mother look after a pack of hounds in Oxfordshire during the war. After that, he hunted four different packs over a period of twenty-six years and, since 1992, involved himself with the politics of hunting, writing submissions for the Burns Inquiry and sitting through all 700 hours of the parliamentary debates.

Brian delighted in seeing foxes. He warmly told a story of an amazing moment when cubs ran over the top of his legs in a ditch in Leicestershire, and a fox that ran up a chimney in a derelict house in Ireland. He told me he would pull up snares to protect foxes if he ever found them in hunting country and once let a fox get away at a big New Year's Day meet. The fox had scampered up a willow tree and, with respect to the fox's guile, he pulled the hounds away and told the remaining hunters to wish the fox a 'happy new year'.

He's an animal-lover in general, and also talked of the joys of working with the hounds. 'To go down the road with seventeen or eighteen hounds who all give the impression that they love you is very moving,' explained Brian.

Roger Scruton also spoke of his love of foxes. He kept a family of foxes on his farm, not just for hunting but because he enjoyed having them around. 'They are beautiful things,' he said. 'We've got a covert that we keep for them. We know that the price of this is that we lose the chickens once a year but it's a price we are prepared to pay.'

Anti-hunting critics would argue that the idea that fox hunters could love the animals is a downright nonsense, and the idea of the hunter's respect for the fox is certainly an intriguing concept to get one's head around. But, although some hunters do despise foxes, it's common. Andrew Cook, the local Master of Foxhounds, who had observed more foxes than most, explained how much he respected his quarry: 'People will think that sounds mad but most purist fox hunters spend half the year hunting foxes and half the year preserving them. I like to see foxes about.'

The anthropologist Garry Marvin noted the notion of care and respect in his accounts of hunting culture. 'Certainly the hunt people I work with have enormous respect for the fox and they wouldn't hunt it if they didn't.'

It might tie in with a tradition found in other hunting cultures, in which a sense of atonement, respect for the life taken and an undercurrent of guilt can often be found. In some African tribes, the hunters must undergo acts of purification following the act of animal slaughter; in others, forgiveness must be begged from the animal to avoid a grudge; and Moi folklore includes tales of hunters suffering because they haven't made the necessary restitution. Those who take part in fox hunting say they don't feel any guilt; but perhaps respect and love for a worthy foe – the concoction of the fox as exceptionally fast, clever, brave or sporting – is similar to the ceremonial rituals in which other hunting cultures engage.

After hearing all of the arguments for and against and all the potent emotions the hunt inspires, I was keen to experience it for myself, to see if I could ever understand the urge to hunt, and why it was so adored and fiercely protected.

I emailed some of the friendly-looking groups that welcomed visitors. 'Visitors and newcomers are always welcome at the Kimblewick Hunt with prior permission from the Secretaries,' said one website. I looked to see if they welcomed foot followers. 'Equally, if you wish to come on foot, the Secretaries will be happy to recommend a good viewing day or, for the fitter foot follower, a good running day!' Bingo.

'We hunt within the law in the south east of England,' proclaimed the website – and I was keen to find out if people still benefited from hunting as a social occasion and outdoor pursuit, following hounds hunting a fox-based scent instead of the actual animal. I was told my request would be discussed with the senior master and they would let me know in a couple of weeks. Eventually, a reply: my request was turned down. I'd emailed a few other hunts in the areas around London – Essex and Kent – as well as a foxhound foot pack in Cumbria, but had had no replies so far. Garry Marvin had warned me that the hunting world was closed. But I persevered, and found a fell pack that agreed to welcome me, the Blencathra Foxhounds.

Dawn took a couple of hours to unfurl as I made my way inland from Galloway to the Lake District to reach the meet. The sea mist cleared to reveal smudges of sheep and the sun began to peek through like the glowing filament of a light bulb. Over the River Nith, the mist returned, and again as I crossed the rivers Annan, Urr, Tarf, Esk, Eden and Kirtle Water. As the sky enflamed with peach, the crows on wires and arrows of pink-footed geese looked stronger. Ponies and pylons, spiderwebs on gorse, were bathed in the early rose light. The colours of both the sky and the land, trees ochre and crimson, were rich, varied and heady: border countryside at its finest.

When I arrived at the venue, the air was gin clear, and people milled around, chatting and catching up. The Master, Michael Thompson, welcomed me warmly, saying they received lots of visitors to the Blencathra, because of its history since the early nineteenth century, and were happy to do so. The atmosphere was one of jollity, friendship and dogs. The Master wore a red waistcoat and green tweeds and had a smiley face. We gathered at the foothills of Carrock Fell, near a pretty bridge and brook. The foxhounds were let out of the vehicle by Barry Todhunter, a well-known and aptly named huntsman of over four decades with impressive sideburns. The crowd of around eighty people gathered to listen to the Master as the hounds snuffled around. A couple of children were there, but mostly it was people in their fifties, sixties and seventies, including a high court judge on his first day hunting in ten years as his tenure was coming to an end. 'A drag trail has been laid down this morning,' explained Thompson to the group. I picked up scraps of the rest of his speech over the crying of the hounds, and confirmed later that the scent was fox-based. 'If a fox intervenes, Barry will control the hounds with his horn. That is not our intention. It is our responsibility to manage our activity.' He told the group to expect a police presence. Some 'antis' – what those who are anti-hunting are called by the pro-hunt side – had been spotted, and I later found out that a local called 'Biggles' who was anti-hunt might have rung the police to warn them of illegal activity. 'Have a great day out,' Thompson said, with a grin and the group sporadically dispersed.

A friendly woman in her early twenties and her father offered me a lift to the side of the hill, where we watched the hounds try to catch the scent. For quite a while. And some. I thought we'd be chasing after the hounds, but everyone was happy to stand by the side of the road and chat. It was low key, stationary and highly social. We had a good view of Barry and the pack and at one point I saw a fox. It was a pale-coloured creature, more gold than copper, but still an attractive blaze of colour against the lead minerals of the rough stone terrain. It soon managed to get away and disappeared into a forested area. For whatever reason, the hounds struggled to pick up the scent of the drag trail, but it was fun to watch them move around the beautiful mountain, and hear them occasionally cry, or 'speak'.

How often do they actually catch a fox at the Blencathra, I asked one gentleman. About one in a hundred, he estimated. I asked another spectator how the ban had affected the farming community, wondering whether a greater number of foxes meant fewer lambs. He said not much at all. I got the impression that it wasn't really about killing foxes, it was more about watching the hounds and getting together. Talk often turned to the 'antis' and how aggressive their balaclavas could make them look but I saw little sign of any saboteurs, though apparently there was one on a bicycle nearby. Sabs also tended to turn out on the bigger meets, such as New Year's Day, as they had done for decades. Despite the absence of any foxes, lots of people I spoke to expressed their love for the animal. 'I love foxes, they're beautiful creatures,' said one, 'but they are vermin.' The ambiguity was alive and well.

We walked to another spot to get a better view and I spoke with a woman who'd hunted with the Blencathra for decades. I made the grievous error of referring to the pack as 'dogs' and she looked sharply at me, raised her eyebrows, corrected me with a cold stare – 'harrrnds' – and physically moved a metre away. Perhaps she thought I was an under-cover sab. Whoops. I was also instructed to stop pointing when I saw the fox, as that would give the 'antis' a sign that a fox was about. The fox is referred to as 'matey boy' or 'Kenny' instead of 'fox' for the same reason. (I was told 'Charlie' was too southern, another faux pas.)

At one point a cry went up, which suggested they'd got another 'line', but nothing came of it. We moved around the mountain again and joined up with a couple of local Cumbrians who were keen to talk about foxes. They tag-teamed stories of cunning from over the years: the fox that ran across the wall, the fox that climbed the tree, the fox that waited in the gorse for the hounds to run past before returning straight back the way it came, the fox that swam through a river before sauntering calmly across the front lawn of a manor house, the fox that swam with a piece of grass in his mouth to drown fleas. 'I'll never forget that fox as long as I live,' said one of the men. They laughed and joked. We discussed accounts of people driving town foxes into the country and releasing them, something I'd read was true but also read was false, and they told me they'd heard of it happening in real life. It wouldn't be fun to hunt a fox if he wasn't so clever, they said, amid delight in the animal's adaptability and resourcefulness. Another joked that the best fox was one 200 metres in front of a pack of hounds.

I walked away realising how the different degrees of separation – fox, master, hounds, people – make it much easier for the hunt to be about things other than killing foxes. The fox is almost the occasional collateral damage of a good day out, at the Blencathra at least. The social coding – the vocabulary, naming devices, equipment, costumes – is crucial for elevating the sport, which is, essentially, animals watching animals sniffing out for animals. The group was mixed: it wasn't just 'toff' types at all; farmhands stood with high court judges, lawyers with bartenders. The fox was called 'vermin' by different people, but the day didn't feel as though the focus was protecting local farmers' lambs and poultry, or an exercise in blood lust. It was more about the pleasure gained in watching Barry and the hounds have a good workout. I imagine from an aesthetic point of view it's much more exciting to watch a line of white hounds on the grey scree chasing the orange flame of a fox, rather than chasing an invisible scent, as it would be if you were watching a predator stalking its prey in a David Attenborough documentary. It was also a walking hunt, and I can only imagine the thrill on horseback is much greater.

Some of the people who most interested me in the

fox-hunting debate were those who started on one side and switched to the other. What factors combine to make someone turn from the right to the left, from faithful to faithless, from sceptic to believer?

Jim Barrington is an interesting character. The former chief executive of the League Against Cruel Sports switched sides and became a consultant to the Countryside Alliance and researcher for the pro-hunt Labour peer Baroness Golding. He supports hunting – although he doesn't hunt himself – because he believes it is necessary for animal welfare reasons.

Jim's conversion wasn't Damascene. He describes it as a slow learning process that started when he began to ask questions about what would happen to foxes after a ban. 'When you're told to shut up about things like that you think, well, hang on a minute, it's a relevant question. What *will* happen afterwards? This is not like badger baiting or dog fighting which are cruel acts in themselves which have no consequences other than a good consequence if you stop them. There'll be things that move in to take the place. If it's all better: fine, you've done a good job. If it's not, then it's questionable. I came to the conclusion that it wouldn't actually be better for the fox.' He was referring to the concern that foxes would still be killed in rural areas, and, if they weren't killed during a hunt, the methods of control would be much less humane, in Jim's opinion.

In the absence of wolves, and other predators, Jim believes that hunting rebalances the food chain, even though wolves only occasionally eat foxes. He also says that foxes with illnesses, disease and injury might become opportunists and go for a chicken or lamb, instead of chasing a rabbit. One might presume that catching the old, weak and sick foxes – as hunts and hunt supporters may claim to do – wouldn't help farmers losing livestock, if one imagines that the stronger foxes would be better at catching and killing other animals. However, according to the Burns Inquiry report, it is widely believed by shepherds that old and injured foxes are more likely to take lambs. Hunting, Jim continued, takes the right ones out, whereas shooting might take out a pregnant or nursing vixen.

Jim, however, is adamant that hunting is not killing just for fun. 'Nothing should be killed for fun, I am opposed to it,' he said, and compared himself with the founder of the RSPCA, Richard Martin, who was a fox hunter. 'Killing to hunt is very different to baiting for torture, which is killing for fun. Hunting has utilitarian value, which is about the population being limited and keeping the population healthy. That's what wildlife management is all about.'

Jim found himself convinced by the wildlife management arguments, but on the other side of the coin, there are those who have switched their support to the anti-fox-hunting groups. Clifford Pellow, a huntsman and kennelman for twenty-three years in England and Wales, blooded when he was four years old, was an example of a pro-hunt supporter who switched sides. 'In the end I got sick of all the killing and gross cruelty,' he told Wales Online, and now campaigns for the League. 'I am totally ashamed at my cruelty to those animals. It's quite awful, quite barbaric really. What I myself did was quite awful.' He detailed incidents of cruelty and stated that it was a nonsense and a lie to suggest that hunting was an efficient method of pest control.

The young farmer Rebecca Hosking also turned her back on the fox hunting she was brought up with from the age of seven. When she was thirteen, it was decided she was old enough to see her first kill. 'I could hear the fox scream-ing under earth, they shot it and threw it to the hounds. I remember them cutting off the tail, which they offered to me. I refused it and got told off,' she said.

Mortified by what she'd seen, she was still forced to hunt but taught her pony how to 'drop a shoulder', which meant she was thrown off.

Her father's moment of conversion came later with the tame fox Red. 'In that six years we had her the hunt was coming in and around our garden,' said Rebecca. 'All of us realised how petrified this poor little animal was for forty-eight hours after, from the screaming of the hounds. She'd be like a brick for days later, and I realised what persecution these animals had gone under which I used to partake in.'

Her father never allowed hunting on his farm again, which wasn't an easy position to hold. Showing you're fox-friendly in the countryside can invite aggression and harassment, Rebecca said. 'My Dad said he wasn't having a hunt on his land again, and they came in one weekend they knew he was away, dug up an earth, killed the foxes and left them in the field for him to find.'

The debate on hunting continues, and is likely to go on for some time. There is still a sense of injustice among the hunts – and a sanguine feeling that they will get hunting back the way it was. 'The themes prevailing through the conversations and speeches are that the Act is an unacceptable imposition on them contrived by ill-informed urbanites who have a purely social political agenda,' wrote Garry Marvin.

The Countryside Alliance still vehemently opposes the Act, claiming that it doesn't protect foxes or other quarry species and has achieved nothing other than to waste taxpayers' money and police time. Some 250,000 people still turn up at Boxing Day meets, and, as the Alliance says, hunting isn't going anywhere.

And nor is the opposition. One of the strangest stories of January 2016 was the news that Keith Flint, anarchic punk frontman of dance music act The Prodigy, had joined a trail hunt in Essex, where he lives. Following widespread criticism, he wrote on Facebook, 'In regards to a story going around about me right now – yes I live in Essex and have a couple of horses. I went riding with the local trail hunt, it was a ride out and NO ANIMALS WERE HUNTED OR KILLED, so my conscience is clear, it wasn't my thing and I won't be going again.'

This didn't stop the hacker group Anonymous from posting a YouTube video warning the singer to change his ways. The message said: 'It has come to our attention that Keith has a fetish for murdering animals. It has come to our attention that Keith has been rubbing shoulders with Tory criminals, whilst out fox hunting. Who would've thought Keith, of all people, would turn out to be a traitorous fuck wit? Throughout the years The Prodigy made music about rebelling against the establishment. You see Mr Flint, we once had a great deal of respect for you, we admired your art, your RAGE and your vision and your haircut, but now, Anonymous have targeted you with the message because you disgrace what we stand for.'

The debate is filled with vitriol, and violence often ensues. And while the ban may be in place, for the moment at least, anti-hunting groups are convinced that the practice still continues. One group in particular continues to monitor and disrupt the fox hunts, looking out for transgressions, with sometimes controversial methods: the saboteurs.

5

Friends and Foes

erhaps the people who feel most strongly about foxes are the hunt saboteurs. They are dedicated to protecting wildlife from hunting for sport. As well as fox hunting, they fight against grouse shooting and the hunting of mink and other animals. Fox hunting is their busiest area, though. To ensure that the ban on hunting foxes with dogs is upheld, they turn up to monitor any hunts they hear about and make sure the legal drag or trail variety is all that is happening. The subculture started in earnest in the 1960s and continues to this day.

To see foxes and hunting from their side, I travelled to meet Alfie Moon – a pseudonym – the education officer of the Hunt Saboteurs Association (HSA), at the house in Croydon he shared with his partner and son. A St George's flag hung in the window. Smoked tofu and other vegan products sat on the shelves along with a vast array of herbal tea. No milk; pretty much all sabs are ethical vegans and view all lives as equally precious.

Five cats roamed the house and upstairs lived a fourteen-year-old rabbit and a couple of tortoises, Jade and Oscar, who'd been around for most of the last century. At one point, Alfie says he had a hundred rescue animals living in his house. Books by Terry Pratchett and Jeremy Paxman, Mark Haddon's *The Curious Incident of the Dog in the Night-Time* and plenty of films lined the far wall. Alfie had just returned from Normandy where he'd been laying a wreath in memory of his father's friends 'who didn't make it'. He wore combat trousers and a black Hunt Saboteurs Association T-shirt. A long brown ponytail and a smart, trimmed beard made him look a little vulpine. He was tall, with a rugby player's build. When he wasn't working with autistic children – his day job – he spent every waking hour trying to stop people hunting foxes.

'Ever since I became aware of the fact people hunted foxes I have known it was wrong,' he said. 'In my heart of hearts I knew it was wrong the first time I ran into a fox hunt, the Old Surrey and Burstow, on a country lane when I was seventeen. They objected to my bike on the road where they were hunting, backed their dislike of my presence with a riding crop and for me that was it. I had to do something about these people. It immediately became very personal.' Alfie described hunters as though their behaviour was pathological, calling them 'violent, twisted and ill'. Speaking of hunters as having a disorder, sickness or perversion is a common way saboteurs, their supporters and anti-hunting activists express their understanding of the group they are opposed to. Early sabotage banners carried slogans such as

'Watch out, sadist about' or 'Warning, pink pervert at large', referring to the 'pink' (i.e. red) jackets.

Incidentally, the Old Surrey and Burstow was the hunt Winston Churchill was once photographed on around his seventy-fourth birthday, at the meet at Chartwell Farm, the home he shared with his wife Clementine, who also reportedly looked after a couple of fox cubs.

Alfie's politics were influenced by his mother and sister, who were activists in the 1990s and involved in the anti-apartheid movement. He started protesting in the Campaign for Nuclear Disarmament (CND) and 'cut his teeth' at the anti-nuclear protests at Greenham Common. 'I was well into the anti-fascist stuff. You had the National Front literally kicking in the heads of the blacks and Asians and I'm proud to be among the people who stood up against them.'

The animal rights movement was in full force and Alfie eventually decided hunt sabotage was the issue he wanted to focus on: 'A lot of people were trying to do everything and burning themselves out.' Sabotage was the one area of animal rights where you could come face to face with the enemy at work.

'It's effective,' he explained. 'You actually get to see the fruit of your labours. You can carry a placard saying "close down this vivisection laboratory", but you're never going to see the monkey or rabbit, or whatever it is they're torturing.

With hunt sabotage, the elation you feel, I can't describe it, you *have* to come sabbing, you have to save that life, you are walking on air. Usually sabbing's a collaborative thing, but occasionally you get those days when you personally save a life and it is just fantastic. It keeps popping into your mind for days, weeks afterwards. It is just superb, it is something really special knowing that you did that. You are walking on air.'

The hunt sabotage movement began in earnest when a young journalist called John Prestige was commissioned to cover a story in the early 1960s. 'It started with the Devon and Somerset Staghounds, who chased a pregnant hind and killed it in somebody's front garden. It was a horrific thing. It was pregnant, couldn't escape and was absolutely ripped to pieces,' he remembered. John now runs an antique and fine-art valuation business in Brixham, a small fishing town in Devon.

Appalled by what he'd encountered, he got together with some friends to start sabotaging hunts. His parents had brought him up to be interested in nature: 'I've always been a great animal-lover so I abhorred hunting. I realised that at times foxes have to be controlled but to chase them for sport and harry them for miles and miles is disgusting and totally unnecessary.'

His group of early saboteurs quickly became skilled and proficient at disrupting hunts. Mostly, early saboteurs were self-sufficient, but they soon started to rely on support from people who disliked hunting tipping them off about the activities of a local hunt. The League Against Cruel Sports was also an organised and official support. From the 1950s, the League, many of whose members were also saboteurs, began to buy land near hunting 'country', in various areas of Somerset and Devon, to impose a barrier on the sport, particularly on stag hunts. The presence of wardens and patrols meant that hunts had to be careful about trespassing into these wildlife sanctuaries, which were a safe haven for the animals and, later, a kind of base for the saboteurs.

One early sabotage tactic was to go to the kennels the night before and feed the hounds with meat, which was often donated by local butchers who didn't like fox hunting and wanted to support the young rogue activists. 'We'd give them a bloody good feed, as the hunting mob would starve them usually for a couple of days,' John told me. With appetites sated, the hounds would be less enthusiastic in their pursuit of a fox.

It didn't always go swimmingly, however. One night in Darlington, John crept quietly into a kennel with a bag of meat at two o'clock in the morning. The hounds were in a large pen outside, the roof covered with chicken wire. He crawled onto the top of the pen, cut a big hole in it and started to drop the meat in. The hounds ripped the meat apart, sinking their teeth into their supper. But then disaster struck. John fell through the hole into the hungry pack of hounds. 'I got very badly bitten and had to cut myself out of the pen,' he said. 'It was the worst thing that happened to me.'

Apart from accidents like that, John remembered the early group being switched on, motivated and organised, 'like the SAS', everyone bonded by a common purpose. The movement accelerated when they realised how effective they could be. The South Devon meet on Boxing Day 1963 in Torquay was the first meet disrupted by the group. They'd spent time researching horn-blowing and exactly the right sounds that would confuse the hounds and draw them away from the control of the Master. 'We caused absolute mayhem and they had to give up in the end.' The police, he recalled, were utterly bemused.

As well as blowing horns, the saboteurs found a number of different tactics. An important method was using repellent to disguise the scent of the fox. John and his early group developed a chemical formula that would confuse the hounds and put them off the trail of the fox, or whichever quarry they were chasing. It was called 'Chemical X' and took a while to invent because they needed to make sure it was harmless to the animals. Various concoctions have been created over the years, the most effective being those with the most pungent smells, such as aniseed or lemon. Other early tactics included blocking roads to prevent hunt vehicles moving, and smoke canisters or fog-horns to scare animals away and create chaos. Banners and placards of slogans drew attention to the saboteurs' cause, and helped get the message across to any press.

As the organisation grew, the tactics became even more elaborate. If sabs could get to the hunt before it began, they would 'beat' the fox out of a covert or any wooded area using horns and whistles, spray scent around coverts and set false trails. A myriad sounds were learned, using horns or the voice. To confuse and misdirect the hunt, a sab might shout 'halloa' to pretend he or she had seen a fox. Certain saboteurs even learn to imitate the voice of the Master.

The innovations have continued over the years, helped by technology. Video cameras are a crucial part of sab equipment, to film what's happening and warn the hunt that they're recording. Footage of any aggressive behaviour or harm to animals is then posted online, on YouTube or various Facebook groups, or given to the police. Dictaphone-like recording devices carried by sabs play the sounds of a barking pack of hounds or the crack of a whip to confuse. In 2014, sabs even used flying drones to track the Alston Hare Week.

Soon, the early sabotage activities were met with retaliation, particularly at otter hunts. At the Culmstock

Otterhunt at Colyford in 1965, John remembers being attacked by staves: 'They tried to set the car on fire that we were in and one of the sabs was smashed by a pole and his jaw broken. We were taken to court and bound over to keep the peace which we thought was rather unfair.'

Otters had been hunted in Britain for centuries, for their fur, for sport and because fishermen thought they preyed on trout and salmon (in fact they prefer slow-moving fish like pike and eels, as well as eggs, frogs, crabs and insects). As opposition increased through the 1960s, the hunting community clung firmly to its sport, which filled the gap in the fox-hunting season between April and November. (A break happened traditionally to allow crops to grow, and when the harvest was gathered in the autumn hunting resumed. The window allowed foxes to breed and look after their cubs at a time when they were scarce.) In the late 1960s, there were eleven organised otter-hunting groups in the country, and in the five years between 1958 and 1963, they killed 1,065 otters. Even when it was known that the species was in dramatic decline, and they were useful, not harmful, to river-based ecosystems, hunts continued to kill otters, with 23 dead in 1971. In 1978, otter hunting was banned, and numbers have rebounded since the species was nearly wiped out in certain areas.

One reason why otter hunts were more dangerous to sabotage than fox hunts was because they were on foot instead of on horseback, so there would be direct contact and conflict between the two sides. Otter hunting was also popular with terriermen and badger-diggers who were part of a culture that was prone to violence. It was described as 'the most vicious element in the spectrum of blood sports' by Mike Huskisson, a hunt saboteur and writer who went under cover in the hunting world for his book *Outfoxed*. It is said that hunts also employed groups of farm labourers to attack the saboteurs.

'We were very successful at stopping otter hunts, but we did have a lot of violence against us, as many as 200 people would come and attack us,' said John.

He realised that if he was caught again he would end up in court and possibly in prison. He felt that 'a lot of people that hunt were the ruling classes, the judges, magistrates and old boys' brigade, who have a lot of influence'. Added to this he saw that the HSA was starting to get politicised. 'I did it for the animals, not because I was a left-wing socialist who hated people who hunted, but we got a lot of people like that infiltrating who had a political motive rather than a love-of-animals motive and it got worse and worse and out of hand so I slowly eased myself out.'

Since he left, John hasn't really followed the hunting or sab world. He's occasionally given people advice but mostly he just got on with his life as a journalist. He noted that foxes still incite extreme emotions. 'Some people have this strong hatred of them; it's very strange really. The vast majority of people are against hunting but they've demonised foxes again, that they're biting babies and getting into people's houses.'

A fox used to visit John's back garden. His wife would feed it fingers of Kit Kat and at one time it had three cubs and would sleep with them on the lawn. In 2012, when Dawn Scott, with Channel 4 for *Foxes Live: Wild in the City*, tagged a group of foxes to trace them by satellite, one, called Basil, found his way to Brixham. He spent 'most of his time amongst a group of houses by a pretty harbour'.

One night a neighbour called John to tell him about the programme. It turned out the fox was nearby: 'This sounds unbelievable but where was one of them? You'll never believe it. In the bottom of our garden. What kind of a weird coincidence!'

Basil, like John, had chosen, according to the Channel 4 programme, to 'enjoy his days living the quiet life by the coast'. But unknown to the programme creators, he'd chosen a territory near a person who, even if it was just for a small while, had championed the lives of foxes.

Alfie, on the other hand, has stayed with the group. He spoke passionately about sabbing, often erupting into laughter, doing impressions of huntsmen threatening to kill him but switching to solemn matters in an instant. He clearly takes it seriously and has trained people in Britain and Europe for the last thirty years. He has also been hospitalised four times by clashes with hunters. Once, in 1997, on a day he described as 'horrific', the sabotage group he was out with ran into an ambush. 'One of them put a lump of masonry, roughly two and a half bricks, through my skull. It smashed the balance centre of my brain and left me needing six months of balance retraining exercise so I could walk without falling over.' Another man he was with was 'damaged much worse and could never sab again'. Instead of acting as a deterrent, however, the violence Alfie experienced that day made him even more determined to stop people hunting.

No charges were brought against Alfie's attackers because, in his opinion, 'before the hunting ban, the police were on the side of the hunt'. In sabotage literature, there are often mentions of police indifference to the conflict between the two. Before the Hunting Act, it was slightly more straightforward: hunting was completely legal whereas saboteurs would often break the law, particularly relating to aggravated trespass. After the Act, with hunting now illegal, the police's and the sabs' motivations have aligned somewhat. But the law is difficult to uphold or enforce: intention to catch and kill the animal must be proved, and evidence of that nature is hard to gather. If the dogs accidentally reach the fox before the guns, that doesn't prove intention to hunt and kill. Saboteurs want to be there to make sure that never happens. It is impossible to say whether the police really are indifferent, as they rarely speak about sabotage, but it has certainly proved a difficult activity to legislate against.

Conflict between the two sides is common and can often get ugly, resulting in violence and injury. Two sabs called Mike Hill and Tom Warby died in the early 1990s. Hill, aged eighteen, was killed by a Cheshire Beagles hunt trailer and Warby, just fifteen, was run over by a Cambridgeshire Foxhounds horsebox. The deaths were ruled as accidental, which led to many protests from animal rights activists. According to Alfie, hundreds of others have been injured. He told me one of his friends had suffered life-changing injuries while sabbing, and also showed a video of a woman seemingly being ridden over by a mounted huntsman who didn't look back. 'I could go on and on and on,' he said.

Alfie points to scars on his arms, where the skin puckers and welts, caused by contact with a spade and a sharpened stave. 'It's only a couple of years since I last got my head kicked in, in Lewes in Sussex. I knew the name of the people who did the last three attacks and they got away with it.'

Alfie insisted that sabotage wasn't a class war any more. Back in the 1970s and 1980s it was, he said, but now it was more concerned with animal rights than politics. It echoed what Dave Wetton, one of the early sabs and the chairman for a while of the HSA, had said. He made the argument that if they wanted to mess up 'toff' activities they'd just go to the Henley Regatta, which would be an easier target.

'This will make you cry,' Alfie said, and loaded up a video that showed a fox being disembowelled by dogs. It didn't look like a quick, clean kill at all. He has seen only a dozen kills in thirty years of sabotage, which could be a combination of the fact that hunts don't always kill and effective sabotage. If you don't get in there and save the fox, he said, you're crying. 'Everyone's in tears.'

His philosophy within sabbing – and that of the HSA at large, he said – is not to 'cause trouble or problems'. He doesn't like having 'wildcards' on the sab van, who might be there just to create aggravation. 'If someone is clearly trying to spark confrontation with the hunt, using verbal aggression, you say, "That's not the way we behave."' If they continue to mess around, they'll be left off the midweek text message about Saturday's activities. It's to protect the rest of the group, as a confrontation could cause people to get injured.

Alfie and other sabs get tip-offs from anonymous sources in the countryside who feed them information about hunts. It also involves hanging around the kennels on a Saturday morning, a 'dangerous' place, said Alfie.

The HSA has 41 autonomous groups across the country. There is little structure, and the committee (twelve people involved in publicity, press, merchandise, events, presentations and the website) cannot tell the groups what to do. Some groups have distinct leaders, others will be anarchist. Often groups team up with others. A smaller group will spray repellent to disrupt the hound's potential to smell the fox, and avoid any contact, 'because they're going to be steaming when they find out what you've done'. Certain hunts have a bad reputation for 'extreme violence' said Alfie. 'Some hunts are nuts; they will just attack you on sight,' he claimed.

The aggression isn't all one-sided, though. Convictions for sabs' actions have occurred since the early years as well. And Alfie doesn't deny that sometimes things get physical.

'The law permits you to use reasonable force to defend yourself but there is no definition of what constitutes reasonable,' he explained. 'It varies according to circumstance. If a guy is coming at you with a weapon, if you can run away, you should run away. But if you have no means of escape or one of your companions is getting his head kicked in, it is reasonable to use force.'

Around the time John Prestige left, the HSA had ramped up its membership, placing adverts in *NME*, the *Vegetarian* and *Private Eye*. Recruitment was aided by coverage in the press, both in newspapers and on television. In 1975, a slot on the BBC's *Open Door* programme, a series which gave the public a platform to broadcast, resulted in a postbag of over 3,000 letters. Groups were set up all over the country with AGMs, a committee and a constitution.

At a party following the 1978 AGM, the sabs sang 'We're sabbing' to the tune of Bob Marley's 'Jamming'. Often they would take holidays to Cornwall, where one HSA member had a big house on the cliffs. The group would engage in various actions, such as scampering down to the coast to empty lobsters and crabs back into the sea from pots and buckets. But it was also there, through the 1970s, with the publication of Peter Singer's *Animal Liberation* in 1975, that the saboteurs developed their animal liberation philosophy, discussing such wide-ranging topics as the ethics of owning a pet, whether pubic lice and tapeworms had rights, and the merits of arson as a campaigning tool.

Fuelled by Singer's ideas and those of the animal rights advocate Richard Ryder (who coined the term 'speciesism' to describe the exclusion of animals from the rights given to humans) the HSA, and the wider animal rights movement, began to evolve into something more militant. Hunting vehicles were immobilised so hounds and horses couldn't be moved to the venue; hunt balls were targeted, with marquees damaged and power cables cut; there was an attempt to desecrate the grave of John Peel, the fox-hunting legend of Cumbria. According to Mike Huskisson, his bones weren't touched, contrary to reports, but the headstone was damaged and a fake fox head was put into the grave with a poem: 'John Peel, John Peel come blow on your horn / Come blow till your cruel heart turns blue / No rest for the thousands of foxes you've torn / But at least this one's got the last laugh on you.'

In 1976, the Animal Liberation Front formed and with it an even more extreme form of protest; it included people who had such conviction to fight for the rights of animals that they were happy to break the law, whatever the cost. The ALF's early tactics varied from releasing undercover footage of researchers in a clinic laughing at brain-damaged baboons to moving a dolphin from captivity into the sea. In the 1980s, letter bombs were sent to the four leaders of political parties in the UK, including Prime Minister Margaret Thatcher. In 1984, the ALF claimed it had contaminated Mars bars with rat poison, because Mars was testing on animals. It later said it was a hoax. Even though activists claimed the movement was non-violent, incendiary devices were placed under the cars of researchers, firebombs left in department stores that sold fur, research laboratories vandalised and employees of Huntingdon Life Sciences targeted. The ALF rarely took responsibility for any of these actions, and there were various other groups operating at the time, such as the Animals Rights Militia, the Stop Huntingdon Animal Cruelty and the Animal Abused Society, which might have been involved.

There was a link between the ALF and the HSA with Ronnie Lee and Cliff Goodman being prominent members of both groups. Lee and Goodman had set up the ALF after serving prison sentences for actions against vivisection laboratories and the arson of a seal-culling boat. The association between the two didn't do the HSA any favours, as the often violent actions of the ALF had alienated public support. Critics called them terrorists. Peter Wilkinson, a political scientist and a leading expert in terrorism, called the ALF and the other animal rights groups 'the most serious domestic terrorist threat within the United Kingdom' during a Channel 4 *Dispatches* documentary. Following the film's screening, the filmmaker Graham Hall told the *Mail on Sunday* that he had been kidnapped and the letters ALF branded on his back with an iron.

In modern Britain, ALF activity is now mainly about freeing animals from factory farms, breeding facilities, battery hen factories or shooting estates. The group keep a much lower profile than it did in the late twentieth century. The hunt saboteurs I would meet kept their weekend activities on the quiet from their colleagues, in case of negative judgement.

That's not to say violence on the part of the animal rights movement has completely disappeared. The hunt participants say that they find the saboteurs violent and aggressive – and there have been convictions of assault for both groups. Writing in the *Telegraph* in January 2015, Clive Aslet reported that 'a member of the public, going about a lawful pursuit in the Wiltshire countryside, was battered unconscious by masked thugs wielding iron bars'. He concedes that the 'rough stuff' happens from both groups but says that 'the hot-headed response of a few hunt supporters who have been at the sloe gin is not of the same order of violence as the assaults perpetrated by certain saboteurs'.

Eventually the police suspended the inquiry into the Wiltshire assault due to insufficient evidence. Pro-hunt activists said this was because the perpetrators were wearing balaclavas, and the Countryside Alliance campaigns and petitions for rules against covering the face, as the sabs tend to do. At the time, Tim Bonner of the Countryside Alliance said, 'There have been at least three vicious attacks in recent years where those responsible could not be identified – will it take a death before action is taken to remove this loophole in the law?'

There have been various convictions over the years of saboteurs for breach of the peace and assault. In January 2016, a family of three sabbing on an estate in Perthshire gave video footage to the police of what they said was illegal hunting. Their efforts backfired and they ended up on trial for 'causing fear and alarm' with the parents fined £200 each. The Countryside Alliance regularly reports convictions or assaults on the side of the hunt saboteurs, just as diligently as the HSA does for its side.

After the 2004 hunting ban, it seemed the majority of the HSA activities, especially the more extreme actions, would come to an end. Members planned simply to monitor the hunts – watch and film to make sure the law was being abided by – instead of using traditional sabotage methods. And convictions have occurred through monitoring – for breaching the ban by flushing out a fox to hounds, hare coursing, public order offences and criminal damage. But, said Alfie, the HSA soon felt that the authorities weren't as interested in the law as they'd hoped, and the quality of evidence needed was often beyond their capabilities. For example, it's tricky to show *intent* to chase and kill with a grainy piece of hand-held video footage. So, they went back to old-fashioned sabbing. 'The hunts are blatantly hunting and getting away with it,' Alfie said. 'Well, we're going to stop them.'

In fact, the hunting ban almost killed the HSA because most people thought that as the law had changed the sport must have stopped, and that the hunts just do 'drag hunting', which groups such as the HSA and the League Against Cruel Sports maintain is just a smokescreen. However, after David Cameron announced a vote to repeal the ban in May 2015, the HSA saw a surge of interest in people wanting to get involved. Hundreds signed up and donations increased. Thousands of people are members, but not everyone sabs. Simon Russell, the chair of the HSA, explained that it involves a certain physicality, commitment and bloody-mindedness. Lots of people just donate money to pay for petrol, vans and publicity. A yearly subscription costs £15.

The only thing that would stop Alfie sabotaging, he says, would be getting killed. He longs for a change in the law that removes the exemptions and makes all hunting illegal. According to the Act, 'exempt' hunting includes that which is done for the purpose of 'preventing or reducing serious damage that the wild mammal would otherwise cause' to livestock, game birds or wild birds, crops or fisheries. It must not use more than two dogs, or one dog below ground. In Scotland, hunts are allowed to use dogs to flush out foxes to the guns. The hounds are thus allowed to find them, but not kill them, although of course if the hounds get there before the guns, there is little chance they won't attack the fox. Another exemption is if the animal is being hunted by a bird of prey, which has, apparently, led to hunts heading out with a ceremonial hawk or owl.

'You just need the police to use their powers once, and confiscate all of the vehicles and crush them, confiscate the dogs, a fine for the huntsman. Just once. They'd all stop. They did it with a couple of guys with the hares, crushed the vehicles, and filmed it. There's been a lot of convictions under the Hunting Act but it's normally working-class guys with lurchers,' Alfie says, referring to the people who tend to be involved with hare coursing rather than with fox hunting.

Certainly, in the modern day, police are actively trying to stop hare coursing. Lincolnshire police force, for example, has set up Operation Galileo, a rural wildlife crime unit working to rid the area of the sport. In January 2016, four police in Lincolnshire were photographed beside a crushed Subaru that had been used by two men convicted of hare coursing. The vehicle had subsequently been seized and crushed by court order, and the photo was intended to send a message that such activities are now unacceptable in the county.

The emotions involved with fox politics are intense, and nowhere more extreme than in the dynamic between the hunting and sabotage communities. The war in the countryside between the two sides is just as dramatic as it was before the ban, unbeknown to the average person on the street. Blood is spilled every Saturday up and down the country over the fox.

I wanted to see it for myself.

A few weeks later, I found myself at 3.45 a.m. in a taxi making its way back to East Croydon to join Alfie's group for a day of sabotage. My nerves were taut – I'd learned more about the violence and aggression between hunts and sabs since my first visit – but they loosened slightly when I saw a fox standing on a pavement. It was a slender animal, with a thin coat rendered yellow by the street lights. It stood eerily looking into the road, with its nose turned into the air, as if it was sniffing for food, earthworms or pears maybe. It was silly, perhaps, but it felt like a talisman of some sort, a symbol of good luck for the trip, and calmed my fears.

Alfie collected me and a newcomer from the station and we drove down to meet the rest of the group. As we drove, he talked of the odd relationship between the sabs and the hunt. 'Charlie' and 'Ginger' were the potentially dangerous people to watch out for that day. Learning the names of the huntsmen and their employees was a strategy in itself: 'If you call them by name they're unlikely to hit you afterwards,' he said.

The newcomer, S, was nervous about being arrested, and questioned Alfie about the law and what to do if the police took her away. He cautioned her to say nothing if arrested but if police ordered her to leave the land, to obey orders. 'The only time you'd risk it is if a fox is being chased by hounds right in front of you. You'd get nicked to save the fox,' he said. He advised us not to speak with the coppers. 'And try not to get arrested as the food in police stations is bloody awful.' I hoped I wouldn't be eating my supper in a police cell later that day.

The sabs, as he'd explained, are committed to 'non-violent direct action' and avoid confrontation where possible. Alfie warned us that hunts-people might try to goad or needle the group, but to avoid swearing. 'That's illegal – even a V sign – and they can go to the police with that,' he said.

We met up with the rest of the group as the sky began to illuminate. It was freezing. At this point, we were waiting to find out if a hunt was commencing nearby. People smoked, caught up, laughed and joked. I explained what I was doing and struck up a conversation with a man about a fox family that lived in his garden. It was a friendly, warm but focused atmosphere. A phone rang. Ears pricked up. Another group had found activity at the local kennels. The hounds had left, horseboxes had been spotted and were on the move. We were rolling.

'Cubbing' was the activity the saboteurs were trying to stop. It takes place before the formal season, in September and October. It's often called 'autumn hunting' and is the time when novice horses, hounds and young people are traditionally taught how to hunt. Hunts say they are following a drag scent or exercising their horses and hounds, within the law. Sabs say they are getting out early in the season to teach young hounds how to hunt cubs or juvenile foxes. The aim of anti-hunt monitors and sabs is to film any illegal activity they see or hear, prevent the death of the fox and disrupt the training process of the pack of hounds to render them less effective at hunting on future occasions. Hunts usually take place around 11 a.m., a sociable hour for a Saturday; however, scenting conditions are better earlier in the morning, so the general consensus among sabs is that if 'autumn hunting' is happening at 7 a.m., it is so the hounds can learn how to find a fox.

I was surprised by how high tech and organised the group was. One man, an ex-serviceman, had a go-pro camera strapped to his head, a scarf covering his face and camouflage gear. His friend, another ex-squaddie, had been injured in Afghanistan in 2009, 'gone off the rails' when he returned home and was trying to get his life back on track. He'd discovered hunt sabotage recently because he loved wildlife and wanted to spend his time doing something healthy and positive. He felt let down by the system that governed the Britain he'd fought for, left floundering, disabled and traumatised from the war, without adequate support or help. In his view, the people who hunted represented the system he hated, the government and the establishment. He had a wide, toothy, child-like grin, and checked to see if I was OK throughout the day.

Others held radios or gizmos containing recordings of hounds or horns to confuse the proceedings. We piled into a van with its seats removed and turned into benches. A younger sab in front with piercings and long plaited orange hair was driving, sitting next to an older sab, with a grey beard and a stretched piercing in his earlobe. They were a mix of people, between twenty and sixty years old. A few worked with children with autism, one was a paramedic, another ran an animal rescue centre, there was a teacher, an IT manager. Everyone was keen to make the visitors feel welcome and looked after.

As we drove to the meet, I spoke to H, who had jet-black hair, blue eyes and chalk-like skin. She'd been sabbing for four years and talked of the hope of saving a life. 'We'll look after you, just stay close,' she said. Citronella spray was handed out, the tart, lemony herbal repellent that would mask the scent of a fox if we saw one. Then maps. 'Hostile vehicle!' yelled Alfie, suddenly, as a farm vehicle overtook us. It was starting to get brighter outside and the group was nervous that we'd be spotted and prevented getting to the meet. Blocking by farm vehicles was a regular occurrence, they said, to prevent sabs from getting to the estate where the hunt was taking place.

I was told that the hunt was known for violence and aggression, and P, the young girl in front, expressed concern that there weren't enough of us to take it on. She said it was too dangerous and we should wait for other groups to arrive. The air in the van was heavy with fear and adrenaline. From what I could gather, she had been attacked and hit with a catapult of ball bearings at the same hunt during another season. Her voice was full of anxiety and she was freaking out. We backed into a hidden lane to discuss, and find out how many we would number. After a quick discussion about safety, learning that a few more from another group would be there, the van moved off and we made for the hunt. 'If a hunt is happening, we have to be there,' said B, who'd been sabbing for twenty or so years. A fox's life was in danger.

The van dropped us off and we piled out, walking up a long, straight drive, with idyllic countryside on either side, the dew twinkling. A deer reared its head in the soft gloaming. Having been awake since three o'clock, I found the whole experience taking on a surreal, otherworldly atmosphere. I was in a fugue state and had no idea what to expect when we arrived. I talked with various sabs about their motivation for being there on our way to the action. 'They think they're above the law.' 'The system, they represent the system.' 'The general public don't realise hunting is still going on. It's the same as it always was.'

Suddenly, we walked straight slap-bang into the meet. Enormous thoroughbred horses, grey, black and brown, reminded me of the line in Roger Scruton's book: 'Their buttocks rippling with muscle like the seething wakes of ocean liners.' Steam rose from the horses and, combined with manure, the smell reminded me of my childhood in Scotland. I was transfixed by how beautiful the foxhounds were, with their wagging tails. By how beautiful the scene was. The countryside, the horses, the hounds all together, the dawn mist, the smell of ferns.

No time to stand and watch the dogs and admire their colourings and tails, though. Immediately, the huntsmen started to film the sabs. The sabs started to film the huntsmen. 'Stop filming my child! Stop filming my child!' shouted one of the men. 'I'm not filming your child, I'm filming *you*!' This is something that happened throughout the morning: the sabs film the huntsmen in order to record illegal hunting activity and violence. 'Why do you need to cover your face?' was another common refrain from the huntsmen, directed to those wearing masks. I could see that, as a group, the sabs look intimidating: they wear all black, with boots, and often have camouflage covering their faces and heads. I put my hood up but didn't wear a balaclava. It felt a bit too weird. 'That's a pretty one,' drawled one of the huntsmen, as they stalked past; I stiffened, wishing I'd taken a mask.

As the hunt moved off, we gave chase. The fastest runners at the front radioed back details of which direction the 'field' was headed. The key sound the group was listening out for was the hounds in cry, for that would mean they'd found a fox. They were also looking out for horses circling a covert, which would suggest the hounds had been sent in to hunt a fox. The worst scenario would be to hear the hounds in cry and not to be there to film the actions of the Master of the hunt and whippers-in. According to the law, the hounds should be called away from a fox.

A quad carrying three men, a young boy of about three and a box containing what seemed to be terriers started to follow us around. Although of course it is not illegal to have terriers – perhaps they were just out for a ride – taking them out on a hunt does suggest they are there to dig out a fox. An exemption to the Act states that one dog can be used to flush wild mammals to reduce 'serious damage' to wild or game birds, but that didn't apply to the land we were on. 'We keep a close eye on where the terriermen are with their dogs,' said Simon.

The terriermen were there to tell us to piss off. We were on private land, after all. At one point they tried to block access to a woodland, through which the sabs needed to get as the hunt had been seen at a nearby covert. With four of them, and about twenty-five of us, they were outnumbered, so the sabs, ignoring them and remaining silent and without eye contact, walked through the forest. I remembered what the women in the van had recommended: look behind you every few paces and face any quads head on to avoid getting hurt. I heard a commotion behind me – I had been told that low-level pushing and shoving was pretty normal at a hunt – and looked back. One of the sabs, G, had been punched in the face from the side. He was bleeding. Immediately, Simon called the police to report the crime. He had been sabotaging hunts for years, and hospitalised at least seven times. In the 1990s, his leg was broken when a baseball bat hit his knee cap. He was unfazed by the assault. Bloodshed really seemed to be the norm when sabbing, something expected and accepted.

The terriermen continued to pursue us, although the man who'd made the assault disappeared. I was later told that he'd pleaded guilty to assault and received a police warning. 'Look back every dozen steps,' I was advised, again. 'They target women so just keep looking back.' Adrenaline pumped through my veins. What the hell was I doing here? I stayed to the edge of the lanes knowing that sabs had been run over both by vehicles and by galloping horses. We made it through the wood and had to cross barbed wire and a stream to get to the field. Inexperienced at crossing barbed wire fences, I was helped to leap over by about five people. I landed on my ankle and it twisted. Bollocks. Fuck, fuck. Bollocks. This would not be the best time to sprain my ankle. I took a deep breath, looked to the sky and tried gently to move my foot. I was in the middle of nowhere and there was no way I could find my way back to the van alone. Please, please, don't let it be sprained. I walked gingerly on it. Thank goodness, it was fine. My feet were already completely soaked through, as were my jeans, but the exercise was maintaining some semblance of warmth. And, trust me, it was serious exercise.

I spoke to G, the guy who'd been assaulted. He seemed spaced out but not too bothered. It had happened before.

My impression of him was one of gentleness. He had a baby-like face and a shy smile. Someone told me a story of how he'd once tried to rescue a fox straight from a huntsman's arms. The huntsman had then flung it to the hounds to kill it. G seemed to be a bit of a hero for the group.

We continued to pursue the hunt, remaining on their tail for a good hour or so. The terriermen in turn remained on our tail, and we ended up on a large plain next to some farm buildings. The whole thing was essentially a big chase: terriermen after the sabs, sabs after the hunters, hunters after the hounds, hounds after the fox, fox after . . . survival.

The police had turned up. They'd been called by the hunt to get us off the land. A policeman, who looked somewhat bored, as though this was a pretty regular, tedious occurrence for him, too, wanted to find out what our plan was. When told about the assault, he said the man could call the station and make a complaint. The perception among the sabs was that the police didn't care about the assault and if it had been the other way around – a sab hitting a huntsman – all hell would have broken loose. It's impossible to say if that was true or not; the police seemed to be trying to keep the peace, and their numbers kept increasing through the morning.

'They're doing what they're doing and finding you guys intimidating,' said the policeman. 'At the end of the day we want them off the land,' said one of the terriermen. 'If they're not killing foxes . . .' said the policeman. A hunter said they were just 'exercising the horses'. The sabs explained they wanted to make sure they weren't hunting illegally. More police arrived at this point. I counted twelve in total through the day. Later, Simon said to me that he thought that police turn a blind eye to violence against saboteurs because they're activists, and that 'if you go out on a protest you deserve everything you get, the mental attitude that anyone who dares to put themselves out there, anything that happens, that's just tough'. Certainly, there are injuries or assaults occurring in the countryside that don't always result in convictions, but the reason for that could be because there's insufficient evidence.

I looked up, and the hunt and majority of the sabs had suddenly moved off. They were about 30 metres away from where I was standing. I began to follow but was pulled back by one of the policemen, who commanded me to stay. I didn't want to be kept there without the female sabs I felt safe around so I tried to wander off nonchalantly – I'm not particularly well versed in slipping away from law enforcement – but the policeman called me back. 'Miss. Miss!' I remembered what Alfie had said in the car earlier: if they tell you not to be on private land, they can arrest you if you remain. I weighed up being arrested against being left alone, but when I looked back, I saw a couple of other sabs had also stayed behind, and figured I'd try to ask the terriermen a few questions instead. Unsurprisingly, they weren't that keen to talk to me.

Eventually we were able to slip off on a footpath to find the rest of the group. The hunt had been called off. The sabs walked back to make sure the hounds were in their van going towards the kennels. Once the horses were put back in their boxes, it meant the hunt was definitely over. Sometimes, the sabs said, they would return and hunt in the afternoon, but it was unlikely. A sab filmed what seemed to be the landowner bringing out a tray of tea for the police. They declined and she walked away. I stood and listened to the chatter, which moved through Jeremy Corbyn's winning the Labour leadership election to Kerry McCarthy, the new vegan shadow environment minister, the perceived police bias against the sabs and other hunts that had been successfully stopped.

From the sabs' point of view, the day had been a success: cubbing had been prevented, no foxes had been killed and, apart from one assault, no one was seriously hurt. It was a victorious day out. On the other side, I don't know if the hunt was hunting illegally or not, but there seemed to me to be an atmosphere of disappointment and frustration, with lots of long faces. Perhaps they were just annoyed that there was a gang of unwanted, balaclava-wearing guests on the land. But although we might have looked unsightly and intimidating, the sabs weren't physically preventing any riding or causing any harm, so if the hunt was just to exercise the horses and hounds, it seemed like a pretty gorgeous place to do it.

We walked out, tired, limbs wet and aching, to where the vehicles had been brought around. Tupperware boxes of banana bread, shortbread and chocolate fairy cakes emerged (vegan, of course) and the group posed for a photograph. I felt completely knackered and could barely see straight at that point. It was a hell of a lot to take in. What was clear to me was, first, how effective hunt sabotage could be at shutting down a hunt; second, that violence is taking place in the countryside every weekend unbeknown to the general public; third, there are probably a lot more police hours spent keeping the two groups apart than people realise – and taxes spent on it.

When I arrived back in London, I headed through Victoria Station and stopped at the shop Lush to buy a bath bomb with salt or something similar for my muscles. I was covered in mud and wet through. The sales assistant looked at me askance and asked what I'd been doing. Lush is known for its animal rights campaigns, and has campaigned regularly against fox hunting, leading to criticism and calls from the Countryside Alliance for hunt supporters to boycott their shops. 'I think you'll probably quite like where I've been, to be honest,' I said. For my efforts, he gave me the bath bomb on the house.

For the moment, it looks as though the conflict between the hunts and the sabs is set to continue, with both sides determined to carry out their conflicting activities. We don't hear about it in the press much, but the violence in the countryside is certainly taking place. That's not to say the fox is out of the media though – it's a big topic, thanks in part to the appearance of the urban fox over the last few decades. As city-dwellers have suddenly got up close and personal with the fox, we've seen a whole new set of con-flicting opinions and interests arise.

6

The Fox Next Door

I often spy foxes on the railway track near my house. Sometimes that flash of fur turns out to be a cat, but this particular day, the animal on the railway track was unequivocally a fox. It was a hefty specimen, sitting proud and tall, unafraid in the bright light of day. In a bush on my right, a loud blitz of blue tits was distracting and I wondered if the fox had registered their lemony breasts as prey. He stared straight at me and I held his gaze for a number of minutes. It was as though we were playing a game to see who would look away first. Eventually he sloped off, up the bank, but continued to turn around and look at me every few seconds. It was exhilarating to feel connected to this wild animal. His brush was full and heavy with a dirty white tip on the end; the rest of his pellage was a rusty brown. He settled on the side of the bank, in among the brambles and weeds, and scratched his neck with one of his legs, eyes closed, basking in the sunshine.

These days, you would probably shrug if someone told you they saw a fox in central London; they are ubiquitous in the capital, appearing even in the most unlikely of places. In 2011, a particularly resourceful fox (nicknamed Romeo by the staff) was found living right at the top of the Shard, 288 metres up Europe's tallest skyscraper. The story captured the city's imagination and was reported widely. 'We explained to him [Romeo] that if foxes were meant to be 72 storeys off the ground, they would have evolved wings,' said Ted Burden, of the Riverside Animal Centre in Wallington. Others have been spotted using the elevators of the London Underground or even riding a train carriage. With this in mind, it is perhaps unsurprising that when a picture circulated online in 2014 of a fox queuing at a cash machine, many didn't doubt its authenticity (it was later revealed as a hoax). Foxes are as much a part of the landscape in London as red phone boxes, black 'beetle' taxis, the sun rising and the sun setting.

Although foxes live in many towns in the northern hemisphere, no other country has the population of urban foxes with the kind of sprawling range that Britain does. Apparently there is only a handful in Paris, according to a 2012 news report in the French English-language newspaper the *Connexion*, following an anti-rabies cull in the 1990s. Their presence in built-up areas is very much a modern phenomenon. After the Second World War, they started to be spotted in the gardens of south London suburbia. In the late 1950s, the Natural History Society recorded that foxes were common in parts of London. In the 1960s, they were colonising the more built-up districts. In 1965, the countryside writer and documentary filmmaker Colin Willock started his foreword to the naturalist Brian Vesey-Fitzgerald's *Town Fox, Country Fox* thus: 'To many city-dwellers and not a few countrymen, the idea of seeing a fox three miles from Piccadilly Circus may seem utterly absurd but I assure you that I have done so on many occasions.' By the early 1970s, they were established throughout much of the capital and outer areas.

During the 1980s and 1990s, foxes colonised new towns and cities, such as Cambridge and Norwich, although this expansion was checked by a significant number of deaths from sarcoptic mange, particularly in Bristol. The over-all population is thought to have been stable at 33,000 in Britain since the early 1990s, although there aren't any exact figures. As we've seen, in some cities where food is abun-dant, there can be as many as thirty-seven foxes recorded in an area of a square kilometre.

So why did foxes start appearing in cities in the mid-twentieth century? There are a couple of straightforward reasons. The fox is relatively small, compared with other predators too large to live side by side with humans in the past. It can move about relatively unobtrusively and make its home in secret without attracting much attention, and in a variety of places, from garden sheds to roofs. It is said that there are more than 10,000 foxes living in London, and although we might well come across plenty of them, we're unlikely to spot any sign of a fox's den.

As we have seen, foxes are also more than happy to eat scraps left by humans. A study in Bristol suggested that on each fox territory within the city there is at least 150 times as much food available as is needed by one fox. Foxes are also incredibly adaptable to new environments and will adjust their patterns and behaviours according to the weather, human activity, prey population, hour of the day and month of the year. Zoologist David Macdonald found that the 'degree of ecological plasticity was unparalleled for a carnivore of this size'.

This doesn't explain, though, why it took foxes so long to make the jump from rural to urban living. After all, towns and cities have been a part of our landscape for millennia. Two fox experts, Stephen Harris and Phil Baker, believe it is down to the way the suburbs trailed out into the countryside during the years between the First and Second World Wars, making a low-density sprawl that provided an ideal habitat for foxes. Typical new-build houses in suburban areas had large gardens with enough space, and often sheds, to offer the perfect homes to fox families. The suburbs then acted as a bridge between town and country, allowing foxes to gradually penetrate further into the built-up centres of our cities.

So, in the 1940s, following the Second World War, although most fox-related mentions in newspapers still concerned hunting or adverts for fur, reports of foxes in urban areas also start to creep in. In 1946, it was reported by the *Daily Mail* that a Mr Mattock of Southgate, a suburb of North London, had trapped three foxes in the run in his garden. In a short item published in the same paper in 1949, it was reported that Birmingham's chief constable had sent out a notice informing residents that 'the only way to protect their poultry from foxes is to keep them in firmly fenced runs'.

These early reports were often neutral, expressing no particular opinion regarding the new presence of the fox – in some cases they were even positive. In 1957, a piece in the *Mail* suggested that the fox was a 'public benefactor' on account of its eating wood mice, rats and beetles. The following year, a news piece ran about a man called Mr John Isitt, who kept a fox as a pet in Stockwell, London, with the jokey pay-off that it was partial to roast lamb and Yorkshire pudding. The first mention of the phrase 'urban foxes' I could find appeared as the headline of an article in the *Daily Mail*, in January 1963, which simply reported 'Hungry foxes hunting for food have been seen in gardens at Exeter, Devon, and Eastbourne, Sussex.'

Chris Packham remembered the perception of foxes in the 1960s when they started to arrive in towns and cities as positive and welcoming. 'When I was a kid in the sixties and early seventies the urban fox was an animal we all championed,' he said. 'It was a hero. We've got them living amongst us! We saw a fox last night! My dad would come and say, "Brian from work's got a fox in his garden."'

The interest in foxes spread to sitting rooms when the BBC's flagship wildlife television programme *Wildlife on One* featured a documentary called *Fox Watch* with Stephen Harris in 1979. 'Everyone loved it,' said Chris.

In 1981, the *Mail* ran an account of a local railway station in Essex having been taken over by a young fox, described as being 'well fed' and 'sleek'. 'It seems only a matter of time before it hitches a ride in the guard's van,' ends the piece, with what feels like a benign wink. In 1994, an article entitled 'In praise of the unbeatable fox' was published in the *Daily Mail*. The initiative of the fox raiding dustbins is celebrated in the piece and the writer ends with: 'This is a most beautiful and appealing animal, and it has survived every sling and arrow man has sent its way.'

There were of course negative reports of their encroachment into the urban landscape. In a humorous article in the *Daily Express* in 1963, the fox is accused of stealing fish on the South Coast from anglers. The journalist wrote that local opinion was already split between those who welcomed foxes and those who wanted them killed. In 1975, the *Mirror* warned its readers to keep their outdoor hutches and aviaries secure at night and printed a picture of a fox footprint. A fox's paw is quite easy to recognise. It is neat and oval, with its toe pads packed very tightly together. Whereas a dog or cat paw print is flatter and rounded, the distinct element in a fox print is its elongated, slimmer shape. By 1977, the *Sunday Times* was presenting a negative profile of the semi-detached suburban Mr Fox, describing him as 'arthritic, skulking under tool sheds, and living off the contents of dustbins and scraps'. An accompanying illustration shows an ill-looking, unattractive cartoon fox with large, sharp teeth, wearing a waistcoat and pin-stripe trousers, with an umbrella to one side, and pointing with one arm to a diminutive-looking tail (the article suggests suburban foxes have shorter tails) and, with the other, to a mangy bald patch on his head.

Part of this dislike for the urban fox in particular is because it is generally believed that there are marked differences between town and country foxes, with the former being painted in an unfavourable light. Urban foxes are sometimes talked about as being mangy, starved, smaller and less healthy than rural foxes. Harris, who has studied urban foxes for decades, says this is not true. In fact, the fox you see on a metropolitan street at night might live in the country and 'commute' into the city to find food, or vice versa. It might even start life in the city but decide to move out to the countryside in later years. Foxes also tend to change in weight and size through the year, distorting our impressions of them. In July, for example, after finding food for the cubs for the last three months, a vixen might look much skinnier. Foxes also moult annually, in spring, and their coats will look a bit thin and ragged, and this is often mistaken for mange.

Hints of the public's attitude can be found on the letters' pages of newspapers. As with the news articles, at first correspondents tended to remark on the fact of the fox being present, rather than complaining or expressing a negative reaction. 'We have foxes at Beckenham . . .' announced B. H. Williams to the *Mail* in 1963, 'only nine miles from Charing Cross.'

Gradually a change becomes visible, as the letters more frequently tend to ask for advice about removing the animals. 'Does anyone know a way to keep foxes out of my garden?' writes Ann Maxwell of Wanstead in London to the *Daily Mail* in 1955. She is worried that they're going to kill her cats. The response suggests a call to the Fox Project, who give advice on fox deterrents. 'Foxes are very timid and usually do no harm,' goes the reply. One intriguing solution from a Mrs K. Bednall of Tonbridge in Kent, in 1997, suggested placing plastic bottles half filled with cold water around the garden, especially at night. The wind will blow into the bottles, making a low whining sound that foxes hate, she said. Another wrote a letter concerned about what would happen if urban foxes got infected with rabies.

This fear over foxes preying on beloved pets is one

of many reasons why the response to this great successful immigration has been divided, but in most cases it is groundless.

When foxes meet dogs or cats they will usually ignore each other. An urban fox's territory might have up to a hundred cats living in it, and mostly they live together without a problem. Occasionally a dog or cat will attack and kill a fox cub, and there have been reports of foxes killing household pets, but this is rare. A study conducted by Stephen Harris in Bristol asked 5,191 homeowners in a high-fox-density area for their experiences. Of 1,225 pet cats, eight had been killed by foxes the year before.

Foxes have been known to take other pets, such as rabbits and tortoises, but if an animal is shut up safely at night, and bolted in a proper cage, the risk is low. Pets are more vulnerable in the spring and summer, when the vixen and dog fox are out and about trying to find food to feed their cubs, and when a pet-owner will be more likely to let their animals run loose in the garden.

We know little about how foxes relate to other wildlife in the city, apart from the fact that they eat rodents, birds, earthworms and insects. Grey squirrels also on occasion, though they are very arduous to catch, bolting up trees and out of reach in a split second. The same goes for pigeons. Little data is available about badgers living in urban areas but if a fox and a badger crossed paths, it's unlikely they would fight. In most areas they live harmoniously side by side. There is a story from an estate in Manchester of a fox and a badger who not only tolerate each other but run around like friends, looking for food and engaging with each other playfully.

It was in the 1990s, however, that a split in public opinion could really be seen, and the balance was decidedly tipped out of the fox's favour, following the first reported incident of a fox injuring a child.

'Horror of the fox that savaged my baby boy' was the headline of an article published in the *Mail* in November 1996. Elena Sheppard had left her son Philip in the conservatory of their South London home for only three minutes when she heard terrified screaming. She rushed in to find the baby's mouth filled with blood where the fox had apparently bitten him on the inside of his lip. There were also scratches on his face. Wildlife experts said they'd never heard of such an incident before. 'This is unprecedented and probably our first recorded incident of a fox attacking a human,' said Matthew Frith of the London Wildlife Trust.

In fact, the first record of such a case was from 1994 when a fox was found on the bed of a four-year-old girl called Renee Prater in a suburb of Nottingham. Donna

Prater, the mother, said the girl had been bitten on her arm. 'It sat staring at us with its horrible red eyes,' the mother told the *Mail*.

In 2002, in Dartford, a baby called Louis Day was attacked by a fox as he slept on the sofa, according to his parents, who said the animal tried to drag the baby out before his father Peter chased it away. At the time, Trevor Williams of the Fox Project was quoted by the BBC as saying, 'I'm absolutely convinced we are looking at a concussed or brain-damaged animal to act in this way.'

After a 2003 incident with a four-year-old girl called Jessica Brown in Tufnell Park, North London, the parents accused the local council of inactivity, having allowed the fox to 'terrorise' the street. The *Mail*'s news story reported that urban fox numbers were on the increase, with many experts believing they were becoming less wary of humans, while an article in the *Sunday Express* declared: 'At last Basil Brush's image has taken a serious dent. Those sweet little foxes who roam the countryside are finally coming out from behind the garbage cans and showing their true colours.'

In 2010, a BBC *Panorama* documentary on the 'fox-attack twins', Isabella and Lola Koupparis, who had been injured by a fox in their cots in east London, drew in 4 million viewers, making it one of the most popular shows on television that month. The incident received widespread press attention with interviews with the girls' parents on other television networks, radio and in print. The fox had supposedly entered the house through the patio doors and climbed two flights of stairs while the parents were watching television. They heard crying on the baby monitor and rushed to the room. The bites to Lola's face had left it 'swollen and distorted'. Her 'eyelid had been badly torn and there was so much bleeding around her eye', her parents feared she would be blind. 'Her arm was open and bits of her flesh were literally, like, just dropping onto Nick's leg. That's how I can remember. It's just . . . it looked like it had been through a cheese grater,' was how her mother described Isabella's arm wounds to the BBC.

Consultant reconstructive surgeon Raj Ragoowansi told the BBC that 'the bite was a very strong bite because as far as the upper arm was concerned the wound was down to the bone and that takes some considerable force to force a laceration through the skin, through the fat, through the muscle and down to bone.'

After the incident, six foxes were trapped in the Koupparis family's garden and killed. Pauline Koupparis said to the BBC, 'We had a police guard on the front door 24/7 for about three or four days and a panic alarm installed in the house because there were lots of things on websites and the tyres had been slashed on the side of the street, and they were just concerned that it could potentially be animal activists.'

These incidents are all labelled as 'attacks', but Stephen Harris suggested that they are more complex than that, writing in *BBC Wildlife* magazine in 2013. A direct attack on a child would look quite different from the cases that have been reported. They would involve bites to the more vulnerable parts of the body, rather than the extremities, such as the finger of a baby bitten in February 2013, said Harris. When foxes come across an unknown object, they will investigate it by sniffing or using their mouth to explore it, he explained. If they don't know what something is, they approach tentatively, reaching out and withdrawing until they work out what effect it will have on them. This investigative, exploring behaviour can of course lead to more severe bites if the fox isn't stopped, but these occasions have been very rare.

The facts around a handful of fox 'attacks' on children are hard to assess though, as some fox experts claim it has been impossible to get hold of forensic records. Chris Packham made the point that no one has died from a fox bite, unlike the many deaths from dog bites in Britain. 'Statistically, it's a nonsense,' he said. 'There are no issues where foxes biting or appearing to bite people end in serious injury or fatality.'

According to the Office for National Statistics, twenty-three deaths following dog attacks were registered in England and Wales from 2006 to 2012. It's estimated that more than 200,000 people are bitten a year, with 7,227 recorded hospitalisations from March 2014 to February 2015, a 56 per cent increase since 2007/2008, and the victims are often young children.

Of course, it is utterly terrifying and upsetting for a parent if their child is mauled by any animal, wild or domestic. Bruce Lindsay-Smith, the pest controller who killed foxes in the garden of the parents of Louis Day, recalled their distress. 'I shot three foxes in their garden. They were in pieces over it. He got accused of making the story up, that it was a dog, but it wasn't, there was no dog there,' he said.

Now and again, these reported incidents lead to a call to cull foxes in cities. Following one case, involving a baby in Bromley in 2013, Boris Johnson called for councils to deal with the 'menace' of urban foxes. 'They may appear cuddly and romantic, but foxes are also a pest and a menace, particularly in our cities,' he told BBC News. 'This must serve as a wake-up call to London's borough leaders, who are responsible for pest control. They must come together, study the data, try to understand why this is becoming such a problem and act quickly to sort it out.'

Between the lack of results from culling in the past and pro-fox groups, a cull was very unlikely ever to materialise, but his comments still served to whip up ideas that the fox was more of a problem than it was. 'When Boris starts banging on about fox populations, I say go to India and spend a few days where there are tigers roaming about. Get a grip, mate,' said Chris Packham.

These calls in favour of culling will undoubtedly rise in number; as the human population increases so too do the opportunities for human–wildlife conflict. A fox-free city would be impossible to make a reality, though. Foxes are tricky to kill in urban areas and there are many of them around, so it is likely that if one is taken out, another will quickly occupy its territory.

Although newspaper articles talk of 'numerous' attacks on children from 'marauding' foxes, incidents of this kind are rare. Dawn Scott pointed to the density of foxes and humans living alongside each other to show how out of proportion these reports were, and that it would be more helpful to ask why these incidents were happening in the first place. 'You've got people crossing paths with foxes every day. If you calculate by probability, the negative incidents with foxes are lower than expected,' she said. 'Any fox showing any sign of aggressive behaviour is blasted all over the newspaper. "That fox is aggressive!" And that's, like, one fox out of how many thousands that are living right next to people every single day?'

In my conversations with people who didn't like foxes, the complaint that they were too audacious often came up. 'I hate them in London because they're too bold and they don't belong here,' said one. 'A fox I saw just stared at me without moving, it was horrible,' said another.

What people might not realise is that if we weren't providing food for them, they wouldn't be there. We have created a perfect habitat for urban populations of foxes. If so many people weren't feeding them in their houses or by hand, we might not have influenced their behaviours.

Lots of people in cities feed foxes without realising that encouraging them into the home or feeding by hand might cause harm to the fox later – or, rarely, to a child or pet. In *Foxes Live*, Dawn Scott found that not only was the rate of people feeding foxes high – as much as 40 per cent of people in Brighton – but once a connection was established, people wanted the connection to be even closer. A city-dweller who starts providing food in the garden might want to get closer and closer to the animal with hand-feeding or encouraging it into the house. As foxes don't understand borders, human boundaries or doors, they will expect to be treated similarly in another house. The fox doesn't see the back door as a territory boundary, Dawn explained; it's just an opportunity for food. The responsibility for the behaviour of foxes becoming bolder or more brazen lies with humans.

'In urban environments, foxes are bombarded by very complex messages by humans and very complex, different types of stimulus and I think we're creating behaviour which is very human driven,' said Dawn.

Bruce Lindsay-Smith mentioned the television show *Springwatch*, the popular BBC series that focuses on the wild-life of Britain, as an example of cuddly nature programming that's changed the way people approach animals: 'It's nature programmes, man's bad waste management, easy access to foods at the back of restaurants – and a lot of restaurants don't care because they have to pay to get rid of the waste.'

Brian May repeated this concern with rubbish in an email to me. 'The slovenly way we live in towns and the lack of ethical disposal of waste has given foxes an image of mere scavengers on human food,' he wrote to me. 'The junk food they have now taken into their diet may have increased their population density, though this is mainly a function of ter-ritory, but it also impacts on their health.'

Another reason why foxes are becoming more habitu-ated to humans might be the fault of irresponsible wildlife rehabilitation centres, suggested Stephen Harris in the *BBC Wildlife* magazine. When an injured or mangy fox is taken in, some centres make an effort not to tame the fox, but others might handle and touch it too much, even though their motives are admirable. If a fox is treated like a pet before being returned to the wild, it might be more likely to trot into houses and eat food out of people's hands, which could lead to a problematic incident or more reasons for people to call in pest controllers with a rifle.

Experts say it is fine to feed foxes at a discreet distance, but taming foxes is only going to cause more problems in the long run. In a way, we are petting foxes to death.

This is a phenomenon that is happening all over the country, not just in urban areas, as a story from 2015 demonstrated. Alconbury is a village in the Cambridgeshire countryside, typical of its kind. Its Sports and Social Club is a busy place, situated near a pretty church which dates back to the twelfth century, close to a winding brook fringed with weeping willows. The research laboratory Huntingdon Life Sciences is just south of the village.

The club was in the news in 2015 after eight of its regulars were 'outfoxed'. One warm evening in June, eight people rose to leave the Sports Club after a night of drinking and socialising to head home when a fox appeared near the front door.

According to news reports, the fox 'trapped' them inside the building. When the gang of friends tried to leave through another door, the 'bushy-tailed bully' ran to that exit instead to pin them inside. Apparently the fox was 'stalking' the customers and bit one woman. Club chairman Bruce Stains, who was chased around the car park, said he had 'never seen anything like it'. Mr Stains told the BBC he 'tweaked his groin' trying to get away. 'None of us could get out. When we tried to use a side door, the fox heard and came haring round there,' he said. One drinker had to use a bicycle to try to keep the animal at bay. Even the pest-control expert was 'forced to beat a retreat' to his vehicle after being pinned in a child's playground, at which point you have to wonder if he was in the right job.

Chris Packham shed some light on the fox's actions. 'The behaviour of the animal was being completely mis-interpreted,' he said, from his home in the New Forest. 'Foxes don't stalk people like that. The only chance that a mammal would behave that way would be if it was rabid but fortunately it wasn't and we don't have that disease in our wider mammal population, thank God.

'The likelihood is that it was an animal who'd been hand-reared that had escaped, was trying to play with people, and looking for food. It's a canid, and they're pur-suit predators, they catch things by stalking them. If I run away from my dogs they'll chase me and start biting my arse. It's the same knee-jerk thing,' he explained.

It is possible that the fox provoked a fight-or-flight response in the victims of the Alconbury incident. As any-one who's been chased by a dog knows, wild animals can trigger primal responses in people, even if the animal is as small as a fox. If the animal's behaviour is unpredictable or unexpected, it can be frightening. The fight-or-flight, or hyperarousal, response is a natural physiological reaction to a perceived threat or attack. Chemicals and hormones are discharged that prepare the animal – human or non-human – either to retaliate or to flee. Foxes may be minuscule compared with wolves, leopards, elephants or other wild animals that live side by side with humans but it is possible that the Alconbury group, similar to parents walking in on a fox in their child's bedroom, experienced a strong physical reaction.

This aside, the colourful words used in reports from British newspapers and websites to describe the fox in Alconbury suggest the fox was displaying behaviours unexplained by its wild nature. The media suggested the fox was a kind of modern Reynard: 'psycho', 'vicious', 'marauding', 'aggressive', 'rampaging', 'angry'. Most people reading these reports would assume there is a degree of hyperbole and comic absurdism taking place, but these words suggested malevolent intent and assigned the animal imagined personality traits. The publication of the stories suggested that it was considered acceptable to do so. You wouldn't describe a wasp as a 'psycho', even though its natural behaviour is disagreeable.

The way this fox was portrayed in the papers is by no means a one-off incident. The British media seem to delight in vilifying the fox. In fact, looking at press reports over the last decade, you would probably conclude that the perception of foxes in urban areas has taken a turn for the worse. The most familiar modern fox characters are that of the urban rascal ransacking bins and fouling gardens, and the murderous sociopath who terrorises homes. This lout has steadily evolved since foxes colonised cities – or humans started moving urban areas into the countryside, depending on how you want to look at it – although the turn of this century saw an accelerated rise in this type of portrayal. One might expect that in a more enlightened, conscious and environmentally aware age, we would have evolved past anthropomorphising the fox, but no, it seems to be practically compulsory.

Other newspaper headlines described foxes as 'marauding', 'vicious' and 'dangerous'. The negative portrayals stretch to other media, too. An ITN video package featured interviews with a couple of people unhappy with the presence of foxes where they lived. One woman said she was 'lucky she didn't get hurt' when she found a fox in her house, after 'shoving it with a mop down the stairs'. Another man recalled seeing 'about twenty-five' foxes in the street, 'congregating around'. He 'didn't know whether to pass them or not'. (To see twenty-five foxes in one place is extraordinary – and very unlikely.)

Occasionally the stories seem to be written in humour. In 2013, a story in *News Shopper*, a local newspaper in Kent, told of 'fox horror' for 'man on toilet': 'Anthony Schofield claims he was quietly going about his business in the little boys' room on July 1 when the mangy creature strutted in before mauling him, his partner and his pet cat,' said the report. 'It was like a struggle for my life,' said Schofield.

A 2011 story in the *Daily Express* portrayed a curious fox in a particularly sinister light. It was headlined: 'Boy just seconds from fox horror in bedroom'. Mother Annette Rook heard her five-year-old screaming in the night and ran into his room to find out what was wrong. A fox was 'skulking in the shadows. Mrs Rook, forty-six, a local junior school headteacher, said, "I was hugging him because I thought he had a bad dream. But then the fox stared back across the bedroom."' The reporter tells us that it happened 'only a few streets from where nine-month-old twins Lola and Isabella Koupparis were savaged in their cots last June'. The twins had 'narrowly escaped death'.

Chris Packham finds this perception of the fox as a dangerous, scary hunter in urban areas particularly worrying. He mentioned a phone-in on a TV show around the time of a high-profile fox incident where one of the listeners said 'she'd been terrified, as a fox had been sat at her patio looking at her grandson licking its lips'. He snorted in derision. 'Aside of being ludicrous in terms of scientific validity, it's embarrassing, because we're talking about an animal which weighs 5 to 7 kilos. It's smaller than a poodle!' In Mumbai, about thirty-five leopards live in astonishingly close proximity to humans, peacefully, for the most part, which puts our fear into perspective.

Part of it, as I knew from sitting in hundreds of news meetings, was that 'fox eats rubbish' isn't a story, but 'twenty-five foxes on street' is, as is 'biggest fox ever' or 'fox bites baby'. Drama rides to the surface in newsrooms especially when it is known that an animal 'transgressing' in a human space will create tension in the reader, and incite them to read more. But whipping up fear in this way isn't helpful – it only succeeds in spreading misinformation, rumour and exaggeration, leading to fears based on what is often complete fiction. In 2012, for example, the *Daily Mail* described the largest fox ever recorded in the UK, found in Aberdeenshire and weighing just over 17 kilograms, as a 'monster'. The fox hadn't done anything except be a bit tubbier than the average fox. Still, it was portrayed as a 'monster' – not just large, but scary – in the headline and two captions.

'Foxes are getting bigger . . . and more deadly,' said an article in the *Mail*, written by pest controller Bruce Lindsay-Smith. 'While city dwellers may silently thrill to the sight of one vaulting over their back wall, they need to wake up to the fact that, unwittingly, we've welcomed a highly efficient killer into our midst,' he concluded.

The actual evidence suggests that foxes are not getting bigger. Of course, foxes do vary in size, and sometimes one will be caught that is larger than average, encouraging the theory that foxes are, as a species, growing. There is an idea of them feasting on the great abundance of food available in towns and cities, with their stature increasing as a result.

There doesn't seem to be much truth in this. It is correct that size and weight can vary according to area: a fox in the colder climes of Scotland might be a little larger than one in the South of England, or perhaps it is just that it has more fur, to keep it warm, which gives the impression it is larger, but any fox much bigger than the average (6.5 kilograms for a fully grown dog fox and 5.5 kilograms for a vixen) is a rare specimen. The biggest fox found in Bristol by Stephen Harris weighed just under 10 kilograms, which is noticeably more than the average for a male fox in Bristol of 6 kilograms, but, he said, foxes come in a range of sizes, and lots of different weights have been recorded. 'We are not seeing urban foxes get any bigger,' Harris told the BBC, following the story of the 17-kilo fox.

One factor that can affect size in the short term is the weather and changing climate, suggested Harris in an article for *BBC Wildlife* magazine. Foxes fare much better in wetter summers, when there are plenty of earthworms to go around, he explained. That is an important determinant in the health of cubs, which are being taught by their parents to fend for themselves. In a hot and dry summer, there are fewer earthworms, and foxes can end up thinner. If climate change continues in the trend of warmer, drier summers, Britain's foxes are likely to become a little smaller.

Being comparatively bigger than your fellow fox is an advantage, especially for young male foxes. Larger and heavier males are more likely to be able to defend and hold on to new territory or win in a fight over a new mate. Heavier dog foxes can also travel further into more territories during dispersal season, whereas smaller foxes tend to father cubs only in their own locale. At the very beginning of life, a larger cub can fight to get the teats that produce the most milk, those near the vixen's groin, gaining more succour and consequently becoming stronger and larger than its siblings, which in turn will give it an advantage when fighting them for any titbits brought home by mother.

A noticeably larger fox will be discovered from time to time, leading to further hue and cry but, as a species, there is no evidence that they are ballooning. The manner in which the media relate these stories, whipping up people's fear and terror of wild animals, is incendiary. Writing 'Mrs Rook fears that the fox was about to sink its razor-sharp teeth into her son's head as he slept' might accelerate the drama of the episode, but a calmer, more factual approach – including mention of fox deterrents, or the reasons why these incidents are happening – will make for a more ecologically literate society.

It's not the media's responsibility to moralise on the rights of animals, but the use of judgemental phrases and fictional colour in news stories about urban foxes is worth remarking. As a news journalist, at college, on a local paper in Maidenhead and then at the *Daily Telegraph* and *NME*, I'd been taught that the basic rule of writing a news story was to make sure no opinion had snuck in there. The most common indication of a new and inexperienced reporter is the insertion of a comment or opinion word that doesn't belong in a news report. Foxes appear to be exempt from this rule. I've already mentioned a few baffling words – 'psycho', 'marauding', 'vicious', 'horrible' – but subtle words such as 'sneaking', 'skulking', 'cunning', 'wary' and 'mangy' crop up repeatedly. In the feature or comment pages, imaginations really run riot. Simon Jenkins referred to a vixen in his garden in an article in the *Evening Standard* as 'a mark one vulpine hipster', who 'glared' at him.

Although these colourful linguistics are present early in the twentieth century – a 'plague of foxes menaced' livestock in Yorkshire in 1943, leading to a village hunt for one particular 'giant', 'killer' fox; the villagers looked for the animal with guns, pikes and sticks but to no avail, and 'The Alsatian', as the fox was known, remained at large – there does seem to have been a marked increase in recent years.

Jessica Groling, an academic at Exeter University, has studied representations of foxes in the media over the last ten to fifteen years. She described these stories as part of a 'moral panic'. She found that a lot of the voices quoted in news stories about urban foxes were dubious and potentially biased sources. The hunting debate was running alongside the urban fox panic at the time, and she found that pro-hunt voices, such as spokespeople from the Countryside Alliance, or the Fieldsports Channel, came up often in news stories about foxes away from rural areas. She saw that there was a vested interest for the pro-hunt lobby to emphasise to urban populations that because hunting had been banned, people were getting what they deserved with an influx of foxes. A kind of 'we told you so' dynamic was operating.

Pest controllers are quoted in news stories with surprising regularity, considering the conflict of interest involved. 'I found it shocking the disproportionate use of pest controllers as reliable sources of fox ecology,' Jessica said. 'Rather than going to people who have written scientific papers about fox-population changes in urban areas, they'd gone to pest controllers to see if they're of the impression that there are more foxes. Obviously pest controllers who are killing more foxes can easily succumb to the misinterpretation that because they're killing more, there are more.'

It might be in the interest of pro-hunt newspapers and media to whip up the idea that there are too many foxes around. Since the years leading up to the Hunting Act, there has been a shift in the debate around hunting discourse away from arguments in favour of hunting for cultural, historic and traditional reasons to the need for hunting to control foxes.

Stephen Harris agrees that the media obsession with foxes is a recent phenomenon. Writing in *BBC Wildlife* magazine, he states that there is a definite link between that obsession and the hunting bans coming into effect across Britain. He believes that the pro-hunting side is using negative media as much as possible to underline the need to control the fox populations, with a view to persuading the government to lift the ban, and the use of the word 'attack' in fox encounters is a useful tool to help get public opinion on their side.

Jessica found a correlation between the political affiliations of newspapers and whether they published anti-fox reports. A newspaper with a pro-fox-hunting, country-sports and rural readership was more likely to run stories that portrayed the urban fox as a menace. I had even heard that during one organised urban fox study, a newspaper had favoured publishing negative reader testimonies about urban foxes over positive. 'They were reinterpreting what are really quite natural forms of behaviour as the behaviour of criminals and deviants,' Jessica explained.

'And they are abnormally powerful given how small the number is,' Trevor Williams said about the hunting classes who might have influence in certain sections of the press.

The result of this kind of journalism is that the fox is portrayed as being impossible to live beside. However, the fear is mainly media centred and media driven. Foxes bring pleasure to the vast majority of the population, according to Dawn Scott's *Foxes Live* data, which found that 86 per cent of city-dwellers like foxes, and 80 per cent agree that seeing them enriches their lives. In 2000, the *BBC Wildlife* magazine ran a poll of 'favourite animals' and the fox came in at second place, after the dolphin. Mumsnet, the online forum for parents to discuss parenting, carries a few threads started by anxious mothers, nervous about foxes spotted in their gardens and whether they will pose a danger to children. On most of the threads, other users reassure the worried poster that foxes pose very little threat to children. In the case of one attack, they asked whether the child might have touched the fox first and recommended contacting a deterrent hotline. The exchanges took place in a soothing and calming atmosphere in contrast to the hysteria in certain sections of the media.

In the depleted landscape that we live in, the fox might be the only animal many people regularly see. For the elderly pensioner who rises at dawn to fix up a bowl of breakfast for a local vixen and her cub, it is a friend. For the clubber, stumbling home at dawn, eyes and ears popping, it is something magical, ethereal, a slip, a trip, that passes at a bus stop – a friend of sorts, too. For the child in the city whose opportunities to experience nature at first hand are limited, it is enchanting and exciting – like seeing snow for the first time, or a steam train. For many, the fox will be the only wild creature that isn't a pet, bird, squirrel or insect that they encounter in their daily lives.

In my own life, a love of nature returned vividly when I went into recovery for a health issue a few years back. For the first time since childhood, I could properly look up and out. Birds appeared. They were suddenly everywhere. I had no idea there were so many birds in London. Clouds of starlings like mosquitos overheard. Poor, maligned pigeons with their oil-slick-coloured coats. Crows! Huge, clever, social, cool, haughty, suspicious crows. Cormorants darting through the skies like winged fountain pens. Along with vision, my hearing returned. The liquid bliss of the blackbird became my soundtrack instead of the music I'd turned to as a sonic opiate. I sought out nature and wildlife like I never had before. A new reverie. 'When you give yourself to places, they give you yourself back,' wrote Rebecca Solnit in *Wanderlust* – and that was my experience.

'I'm interested in the health benefits associated in engagement with wildlife because I think we get a lot we don't realise,' said Dawn. 'That includes things like reducing stress and isolation, which are actually big killers for older people.' Most of the people who fed foxes were elderly, found *Foxes Live*.

Colin Race was one of the people the *Foxes Live* team spoke to. In his mid-thirties, he lived in Hove and worked in the local council archives. He started feeding foxes scraps of food and went into detail about the menu he offered: 'Bread with leftover sauce or jam on it (small bits or it might get stuck to the roof of their mouths), raisins for their sweet teeth, cocktail sausages, sometimes an egg for a special treat.' He was keen to stress he didn't feed his foxes by hand or recommend people try to touch foxes or to entice them to take food from their hands.

The first fox Race got to know was less fearful of him because the animal had mange. 'I'd be out there and talk to him; I spent a lot of time with him,' he said. Colin and the fox became close and attached. 'He was always happy to see me,' he remembered. 'He'd come running down to meet me on the street and taught his cubs to meet me, to get food.' Rolf eventually ran away – he was the fox called 'Fleet' in *Winterwatch* who travelled the equivalent distance of London to Manchester – but soon others appeared for Colin to feed and watch.

One of these was a far shyer animal than the rest, but an accident led him to seek help from Colin, which seems an intelligent, conscious thing to do. 'He broke his leg and he came down with a badger one night and announced himself to me, like, "I need help, can you feed me?" From that day on he was a hundred times friendlier than he'd ever been, out in the open, waiting for the food, after I helped his leg heal up.' The relationship worked both ways and Colin said his life was enriched by it, too.

Anyway, despite the fact some see foxes as a nuisance, a London, for example, without foxes might not be much of an improvement. For a start, foxes keep rodent numbers down. We would certainly see an increase in the number of rats and house mice in our houses if foxes disappeared from our streets and parks. Other species would move in to fill the ecological niche left by the scavengers, so this could mean an increase in gulls and crows. Some people in seaside towns already view seagulls as a problem. The extra food left by the foxes would be eaten by pigeons, rats, mice and other animals, so we would see those populations increase. Perhaps the vegetation in cities would even change for the worse too. It is thought that foxes spread wildflower seeds around different territories, through their fur and faeces. Without this transport, our cities and towns might be a lot less ecologically vibrant.

Across Britain, there is a proliferation of wildlife rehabilitation and rescue centres. These organisations were often set up by one or two people with a personal passion for helping animals and then grew into registered charities. The Fox Project started out as an information centre for councils in London, as we've seen, but these days it is also a place where injured foxes are looked after until they're ready to be released into the wild, and it is proof, if any were needed, that some people in this country love foxes.

June was almost over and summer was making itself at

home, settling in comfortably after the rapid rollercoaster of spring. I wound down the car window to take in the smell of the High Weald in Kent. It is not as wooded as it once was – it was recorded in the Domesday Book in 1086 as England's most forested area – but about two-thirds of the area is ancient woodland. Compared to the rest of our obliterated landscape, that's impressive. The High Weald is home to brown hares, water voles, pipistrelle bats, great crested newts and Devil's bolete, a mushroom with a crimson stubby trunk and a warty, deformed cream hat, a gnome that's been turned into a mushroom by a witch's spell. It's one of many mushrooms with wonderful lyrical names: Soapy Knight, Aromatic Knight, Plums and Custard, Purple Jellydisc, Hairy Earthtongue, Black Witches' Butter, the Flirt. Much of the parkland of the area and nearby Ashdown Forest has been reserved and developed for hunting since the thirteenth century.

As well as being a rare habitat for British wildlife, the High Weald is home to foxes, and the Fox Project's headquarters. I arrived at the building to meet director Sandra Reddy. Blond and bespectacled, she'd dedicated her life to animal rights after being inspired by the films of David Attenborough and Jacques Cousteau. She ran the project from a building rented from the Folly Wildlife Rescue service. We moved into the main room and the overpowering smell of fox hit the back of my throat.

There were a number of spacious cages on one side of the wall with four or so foxes sitting in them. Most were there as a result of traffic accidents or getting caught on fencing, in football nets or in garden ponds without easy-exit beaches. Mandy sat at the back of her cage in the corner. She had a bad infection on her rear leg and was on antibiotics. Her coat was a tawny brown and she had a bright white tip on her brush. She played with a soft toy in her cage listlessly and looked out, wide eyed. Another fox had a much paler orange coat; another a much brighter reddish hue. Tilda was in the hospital because she'd got netting stuck around her hind leg. The other foxes were being treated for mange. They all stared out at us, looking timid, shy and clearly quite unwell. The organisation preferred to give the foxes old-fashioned names such as Doris, Ethel, Neil or Junior instead of prissy names like 'Sweetheart' or 'Princess' as a mark of respect. Each cage was marked with the medical details and the reason why the fox had been brought in.

Giving the foxes names helps with promotion of the work on social media, too. The Facebook page is incredibly popular, with nearly half a million people following it. With each fox, the project posts an update about its welfare, a picture and often a video of it being released into the wild. The comments underneath the posts (mainly from women – the data gathered by *Foxes Live* showed that women do tend to like foxes more than men do) illustrate how many people feel about foxes, and their rehabilitation. Underneath a picture of Junior, who was suffering from mange and an ear infection, and had large ears dappled with cream and dark brown colouring, Joan had written, 'Get well soon, Junior, love you X PS you look so snug, have a nice life sweetie.' A picture of a poorly Neil, recovering after being hit by a car, which had left him with a broken jaw and severe concussion, elicits messages such as 'Bless him, hope he stays away from the roads. Thank you for all your care of him and all the others' and 'Be careful out there Neil x'. Other comments pledged to send food or newspapers or other resources, or hold coffee mornings to raise money for the organisation. 'People love the cute pictures,' said Sandra. 'The foxes speak for themselves. They are gorgeous and adorable.' It clearly helps engagement if there's an image of a fox, even when they look a bit tatty and unwell.

At the time I was there, the hospital had 120 animals in its system, looked after by rescuers dotted around the South East. If a fox is found injured in, say, Chatham, they'll call, say, Jan and see if she can go down and check out the fox. Every day of the year they run twelve-hour shifts with the ambulance and a vet called Ian is on hand to advise on the fox's health when it arrives at the headquarters. The organisation has come a long way over the last couple of decades, from Trevor Williams's makeshift wildlife hospital at his own home with a few cubs to an organisation that rescues around 700 animals a year, including 250 cubs.

Sandra had worked at the Fox Project for fourteen years, following time spent working for Animal Aid. She spoke clearly and calmly, eager to dispel myths. She obviously had a strong love and care for the foxes and became most animated when telling stories about them. She remembered one fox in particular who had to be put to sleep after being shot. 'There was no saving him, he was lying in horrible pain. They do these horrible things away from the public eye so you don't see a lot of it.'

While I stood there talking to Sandra, an injured fox was brought in. Suddenly, everyone sprang into action. 'It was a bit of an adventure getting her,' said Lucy, a staff member with piercings and tattoos, who'd worked at the Fox Project for years. An injection was administered. A wound on the back leg cleaned up. The fox would remain in recovery at the rescue centre until she was well enough to be released into the wild.

'Most of the British public love foxes, when you look at the hunting ban, you've got well over 80 per cent who are pro-fox,' she said, referring to the proportion of people in favour of keeping fox hunting banned, according to an Ipsos MORI poll at the end of 2014. 'The ones who are anti-fox have the biggest mouths and friends in high places, the press, the judges, parliament.'

It is that love of foxes that keeps the Project going. 'We wouldn't be able to do it without members of the public. You hear all the hate stories but when it comes to it people love them or we wouldn't have a job.'

Although negative portrayals of the fox abound in the newspapers, many other forms of media paint them in a positive light, illustrating the way most of the population feels about them. Just as early perceptions of the fox in history were influenced by the stories of Chaucer, Aesop and Reynard the fox, painting the fox as essentially a wicked threat, new representations of the fox introduced a new character through modern media: an animal that's interesting, from a scientific point of view, and both adorable and amusing, a familiar internet meme.

British television has become an important stage for stories about animals. *Zoo Quest* was the first TV show that made legendary British naturalist and broadcaster David Attenborough's name. It aired on the BBC in the 1950s and charted his journey into the Far East to capture animals for London Zoo. From pangolins to komodo dragons, gibbons to baby bears, the exotic was transmitted into people's living rooms for the first time, and nature documentaries have rarely left our screens since. A new David Attenborough show such as *Life*, *Planet Earth*, *Life in the Undergrowth*, for my millennial friends at least, has been a cultural event over the span of our lives.

Attenborough celebrated urban foxes in his own documentary in the 1970s but he also paved the way for a legacy of other TV shows such as *Foxes Live*, Dawn Scott's investigation, and the enduringly popular *Springwatch* franchise, presented by Chris Packham, among many others.

The internet and social media have also spread this love of animals even further. Viewers unite at home in their delight at the creatures on the screen, turning the animals into celebrities. 'Spineless Simon', the stickleback unlucky in love in 2015's *Springwatch*, even had his own Twitter account.

Animals on the internet are digital catnip. BuzzFeed, the major web media success story of the twenty-first century, even has its own Animals Editor. Foxes are very much part of that positive, cute, awed narrative and are guaranteed to bring in page views. A few recent headlines on BuzzFeed include: '21 Adorable Fox Products You Need In Your Life', '18 Reasons Foxes Are The Most Adorable', '18 Fuzzy Foxes Who Will Make You Feel Way Better About Winter' and '17 Happy Foxes Who Are Celebrating The Fox-Hunting Ban'. One would be surprised to see an anti-fox article on one of the modern media outlets such as VICE or BuzzFeed, sites that aren't weighed down by a history of readers who the national print might expect want to read about foxes from a certain angle. The tone of fox-related stories is more 'OMG look at this cute fox!' rather than anything related to the controversial subjects of hunting or population control or culling.

But the most famous fox on the internet is Gus the Fox. He's so famous he's even got his own book, with a foreword by the comedian Noel Fielding. In one of today's leading currencies – Twitter followers – Gus the Fox is relatively rich, with over 100,000. Though he's quieter now, I remember the days when you'd see someone sharing a Gus the Fox comment or picture every day.

Gus the Fox is a kind of absurdist parody of the dirty, stinking, evil, urban-fox character. He killed his own Gran in a fight over sausages and was banished to London. A typical day involves barking at people in wheelchairs, visiting prostitutes for snacks and cuddles, rummaging in bins and making a right pig's ear of someone's driveway. Other activities include shoving frogs down drains, saying things so upsetting that it makes a cormorant's heart explode and punching swans.

People loved Gus the Fox. He was funny, and wittily skewered this strange attitude we have in Britain towards wildlife. Get too close, and you're a 'psycho' fox; migrate with too many other jellyfish at the same time, and you're a 'mutant killer plague'; disperse together as you are designed by nature to do, and you're a 'monster swarm' of flying ants that need to be got rid of. Reports are often much more skewed towards how 'crazy' and 'evil' and 'terrifying' these creatures are instead of towards the facts – that ants, for example, keep our basic ecosystems running, through turning over and oxygenating soils and providing food for other animals. We need them.

The comedian behind Gus the Fox is Matt Haydock – and he'd observed the strange, ambiguous relationship Britain has with its leading predator by portraying a fictional character.

'You go to a shop like Joy or Oliver Bonas and you can buy jumpers with foxes on or jewellery; it's all over the place,' said Haydock. 'But then when you actually talk to people, they're like "Oh, I dunno how I feel about them, maybe we should kill them?" Well, why have you got a big picture of one looking majestic? Why do humans do that?'

What happened to Gus the Fox was interesting. The more Haydock gave a voice to the fox, the more he felt he had a duty to speak out for foxes as a species. His website went from being 'straight-up daft' to more serious. Chris Packham got involved and Haydock started writing about animal welfare issues. 'I changed him from being something ludicrous and farcical into something more serious, which alienated a lot of people,' he said.

Gus the Fox was an early incarnation of the internet animal celebrity and spawned many knock-offs. Although most people who followed him were fans and supporters, Haydock told me he'd received negative, direct tweets from pro-hunting groups, and witnessed the strange dichotomy people display about foxes in this country, in that, as he put it, 'It's OK to like a fox if it's on your ring, but not in real life.'

Dawn Scott is fascinated by trying to work out why some people hate foxes and why others love them. 'I find it quite hard to understand from a personal point of view,' she said, 'so I'm interested in what triggers negativity towards wildlife. If you can understand that, you can hopefully put things in place to reduce that conflict.' In her work delving into the psychology of perception towards 'pest' species using data from questionnaires, she found that if someone had a pet they were found to be more positive towards wildlife in general, but that most people had either a neutral or positive attitude towards a species until they had a bad encounter with it.

'Most people who had negative attitudes had a negative experience: losing a pet, or fox cubs in the garden that they didn't want,' she said. 'The number of people with poultry in the city has grown due to the popularity of sustainable living and they attract foxes and most people don't look after them properly.'

Dawn had worked in countries where the human population lived close to much bigger and more dangerous animals than foxes. Tanzania, for example, where the Masai live with lions. She compared people's tolerance to large predators in places such as Africa with our intolerance to any form of carnivore. Reasons for negative feelings towards foxes in Britain were fear of danger to pets, irritation at foxes digging up the garden, dislike of poo and noise – just as Bruce, the pest controller, had found. This resentment, the idea that 'this is our space, we don't want wildlife here', is, said Dawn, a learned rather than a natural behaviour.

As our conversation continued, she revealed her own admiration for the persecuted animal. 'It's a shame it is the fox,' she said, 'because they are amazingly beautiful. Because they become habituated and people walk past them, they want that animal to be scared and because it's not scared of them, it's not right. We should dominate wildlife, they think.'

After my visit to Dawn's office, I wanted to eat chips on Brighton beach and take a quick sniff of the sea. I sat on the beach and tucked in, the big wheel on the pier spinning gleefully in the distance. In a matter of seconds, I was no longer alone. A surprisingly enormous seagull was about a foot away from me. I could see the lemon yellow of its iris, cool and flat. One seagull quickly became three. Then five, seven, eight. I was surrounded by nine seagulls. They formed a baggy but close circle around me and stared at my chips, transfixed. I continued to eat but recognised a new emotion. It wasn't that I was scared of them - but I felt oddly irritated by their presence. What would it take for a fox to be too wild for me?

Trevor Williams, in his fifty years of watching foxes and dedicating his life to their welfare and rights, thinks that they are so vilified in this country because they are, quite simply, wild. 'People like controlled animals. They like them to be acceptable and predictable. These are dogs which are not willing to be domesticated.' He made comparisons with other wild dogs demonised across the world – dingos in Australia, coyotes in America.

While we categorise most creatures as either livestock, pets, vermin, charismatic species to be saved or ugly species to be ignored, the fox is an example of a wild animal that exists in an ambiguous space. It can be seen as a potential threat. Perhaps the hysterical media reports that abound are just preying on a widespread anxiety that's already present in our society, that when creatures succeed in our urban areas, we are not in complete control. Wild animals are fine if they're in a zoo, in the park or on the television, but in the territories we have designated as human? An offence to many. These reports feed on that psychology of annoyance, disgust and even fear, a potent mix that guarantees head-lines, front pages and high positions in news bulletins and talk shows. 'Some of the demonisation that's taken place in the last ten to fifteen years has been insidious in the extreme and perhaps even malevolent,' said Chris Packham.

Chris once told the *Evening Standard* that he preferred foxes over bigger charismatic carnivores such as tigers. 'In the ruins of the world in which we live, we have an animal that's capable of not just living alongside us, but succeeding,' he said. 'We should champion this animal and think how fortunate we are to have a creature which can adapt and live within our manscape. But we don't, do we? As soon as a creature starts to increase in number, seemingly rational people start to get queasy and go "Oh my God, we must have a cull, there are too many of them."'

'The fox is a badge of our intolerance,' he explained. 'It's time to put these countryside anecdotes behind us and concentrate on science which is currently proven. The idea of foxes in the hen run as psychotic animals, I mean, good God, it's something from the Middle Ages!'

But the fox has been an enemy in culture and folklore much longer than it's been a friend or something to defend. Although it seems to be a small number of people who genuinely dislike the fox, it is possible that the media are feeding off a hard-wired fear in humans of wild animals, and the desire to dominate and survive. Certainly, these primal emotions of fear and anxiety exist to keep us safe – it makes sense as a species to be wary of potential threats.

Perhaps because most interactions people have with foxes in the modern world are virtual, through dramatic stories in the media, those who dislike foxes may assume a higher threat than the reality confirms. If we saw foxes every day, our wariness would probably decrease. In the same way, if we lived side by side with bigger predators, such as leopards or tigers, we would probably be less afraid of foxes.

As Chris Packham put it: 'Maybe we need a beast in the woods because there are no beasts left in the woods. Is the fox contemporary Britain's wolf from *Little Red Riding Hood*?'

This standpoint, that humans are detached from the rest of the natural world, and anything that might challenge manmade harmony needs to be taken out, is damaging to human–animal relations – and to the wider environment. It also forgets that the foxes living in the post-war suburban sprawl, in the space deemed 'human', the space where they 'didn't belong', probably lived there before the cement mixers arrived.

As we can see, the ambiguity of the fox in the modern day is perhaps starker than it ever has been. I've spoken to people willing to risk life and limb to save the fox, and to a hunter who told me that, if she could have her way, she'd kill all the foxes in Britain, so extreme was her hatred. People both loathe and love the animal fiercely, and it stands apart from the rest of British wildlife because of its enemies and friends on both sides. The fox has never been a tabula rasa, but it has become more things to more people since attitudes towards animals shifted in the twentieth century. And with talk of a repeal of the Hunting Act, I very much doubt this will be changing any time soon.

Epilogue

The sun was beginning to set in the late afternoon as I walked home through the park, and I could sense a change in the atmosphere. Quiet. Calm. Peace. Blood slowing. Hummed to stillness by the wild things, the trees and their roots.

It was prime foxing hour in the city so I wandered slowly down my favoured edge: a tree corridor, ridged on one side by a railway track and on the other by a raised part of the park that provides a welcome, rare horizon to soothe the sensory overload. On my left, there were plenty of potential fox earths: large tree roots, bushes, wallows, banks and dips, a fox's wonderland. I paused in the shadows, hoping, as dusk settled, to see a local heading out for its evening meal. Voles, worms or sandwich crusts, perhaps. Leaves clung to the trees like shreds of scrap paper, tatty and ragged. Flurries of *Clematis vitalba*, or old man's beard, were bent over, grey and furry like malnourished wolves. Winter was coming.

As the final squeals of the local parakeets and the bleeps and the clicks of a robin hushed, I continued through the residential roads, peeking through the gaps between parked cars and scouring the tops of fences and walls – I'd recently seen a fox jump up onto a fence that must have been two metres high.

The rising moon was so bright it looked as if it had been freshly born. As my eyes swept the pavements, I spied something furry behind a car wheel. Could it be? Pause. Wait. Still. Holding breath. A fox sauntered out. The body was slender and small, which made its ears look hefty, as if it was yet to grow into them. Perhaps it was a juvenile. The fur on its neck gleamed white in the street lights and the tail looked soft and hung low to the ground. Because of the size and the fineness of the fur, I guessed she might be a young vixen. She seemed relaxed and comfortable; I hadn't frightened her. She was a splendid creature, and, in that moment, I couldn't reconcile the animal in front of me with the nuisance pest it had been seen as for centuries.

While I agree with the argument that foxes should be controlled when necessary to protect rare and vulnerable species, and I also have sympathy for farmers who have lost animals to a hungry fox, the fox's perceived villainy has much to do with our attitude to the earth and the way we treat it. The fox is a problem only in so far as it affects our own interests – and that problem is often exaggerated to suit other agendas. Intentions of spite and malevolence have been projected onto the fox for many years when, in fact, it is simply a wild animal, acting according to its nature.

It must be possible to reorganise our priorities to safeguard the natural world. The idea that we stand apart from other living organisms, that we can exploit them or exclude them from what we deem as our space, doesn't add up to a healthy environment. The fox is in urban spaces only because of our habits; we can't expect to live as we do and not affect the world around us.

We stared at each other, the fox and I, for a charged moment. Her eyes were a pale bronze and seemed bright and aware. She turned away and trotted down the street towards my house. She wasn't in a rush at all. We walked for a while, her in front, me a few paces behind. In those seconds, I got the sense that we were one and the same, that we were both just animals, mammals, predators, denizens of this earth. As she turned a corner, I gave gentle chase but within a few seconds she had leapt up onto a wall and slunk off into the undergrowth. It was an enlivening thrill, as always.

Notes

All quoted material is from interviews or correspondence with the author, unless otherwise noted.

Chapter 1

Page 9, 'I am passionately obsessed . . .'
WETA magazine, March 1990

Page 10, 'It is my little nest, my womb'
Audio tape from Roald Dahl Museum and Story Centre

Page 11, 'It would also hold something of a moral . . .'
Donald Sturrock, *Storyteller: The Authorized Biography of Roald Dahl* (London: Simon & Schuster, 2010)

Page 15, . . . on average only between 46 and 86 centimetres . . .
animals.nationalgeographic.com/animals/mammals/red-fox/

Page 17, The fox's wits are referred to . . .
Martin Wallen, *Fox* (London: Reaktion Books, 2006)

Page 18, Aelian, the Roman author . . . body to the ground
H. G. Lloyd, *The Red Fox* (London: Batsford, 1980)

Page 18, The *Physiologus*, a second-century Christian text . . . and gobbles them up.'
T. H. White, *The Book of Beasts* (Madison: Parallel Press, 2002)

Page 18, In January 2016 the ruse was actually caught on film.
www.youtube.com/watch?v=wh8wPqpIRKc

Page 20, . . . in Britain, the earliest sheep are dated over 5,000 years ago.
Derek Yalden, *The History of British Mammals* (London: T & A D Poyser Ltd, 1999)

Page 20, . . . the oldest fox remains in Britain date back to the Wolstonian period . . .
Yalden, *History of British Mammals*

Page 21, The earliest and clearest account . . . killed by the local fox.
Lloyd, *The Red Fox*

Page 21, Foxes observed in areas in Britain . . .
David Macdonald, *Running with the Fox* (London: Harper Collins, 1989)

Page 25, As Joan Acocella wrote . . .
Joan Acocella, 'Fox News: What the stories of Reynard tell us about ourselves', *New Yorker*, 4 May 2015

Page 25, *On the first day of Spring in the year ninety-three* . . .
Josepha Sherman (ed.), *Storytelling: An Encyclopedia of Mythology and Folklore* (New York: M. E. Sharpe, 2008)

Page 28, . . . to use Colin Willock's phrase, 'splendidly nefarious'.
Brian Vesey-Fitzgerald, *Town Fox, Country Fox* (London: Andre Deutsch, 1965)

Page 30, 'The fox signifies the Devil in this life . . .
Thomas Wright, *Popular Treatises on Science Written During the Middle Ages* (London: 1741)

Page 31, In a scene from a French manuscript . . .
British Library, www.bl.uk/catalogues/illuminatedmanuscripts/ILLUMIN.ASP?Size=mid&IllID=40417

Page 32, The fox is depicted most often as a bishop . . .
Kenneth Varty, *Reynard, Renart, Reinaert and Other Foxes in Medieval England* (Amsterdam: Amsterdam University Press, 1999)

Page 32, The first example of the word 'fox' being used . . . children or persons of bad stock'.
The Oxford English Dictionary, Second edition (Oxford: Clarendon Press, 1989)

Joseph Wright, *English Dialect Dictionary* (Oxford: Oxford University Press, 1898–1905)

Page 36, . . . a study conducted by Claire Marriage . . .
Yalden, *History of British Mammals*

Page 37, In Ancient Britain . . . and their fur.
Stephen Harris and Derek Yalden (eds), *Mammals of the British Isles Handbook* (Southampton: The Mammal Society, 2008)

Page 37, There is a recipe . . . with chestnut pasta.
http://news.bbc.co.uk/1/hi/programmes/the_daily_politics/4853388.stm

Page 38, . . . the rest of the body was removed for its pelt . . .
I. L. Baxter and S. Hamilton-Dyer, 'Foxy in furs?', *Archaeofauna*, vol. 12, pp. 87–94 staffprofiles.bournemouth.ac.uk/display/journal-article/33090#scopus

Page 38, In a 1986 paper . . .
Daniel Maurel et al., 'Seasonal moulting patterns in three fur bearing mammals', *Canadian Journal of Zoology*, vol. 64, no. 8 (1986), pp. 1757–64, www.nrcresearchpress.com/doi/pdf/10.1139/z86-265

Page 39, London became a hive of the fur trade . . .
Anthony Holmes-Walker, *Sixes and Sevens: A Short History of the Skinners' Company* (London: The Skinners' Company, 2005)

Page 39, . . . the royal household commissioned 79,220 skins of trimmed miniver . . .
Elspeth Mary Veale, *The English Fur Trade in the Later Middle Ages* (Oxford: Clarendon Press, 1966)

Page 39, Just one of Henry VI's robes . . .
Roger Lovegrove, *Silent Fields* (Oxford: Oxford University Press, 2007)

Page 39, An essay on the fur trade in the early medieval Mediterranean . . .
James Howard-Johnston, 'Trading in fur from classical antiquity to the early middle ages', in E. Cameron, *Leather and Fur. Aspects of Early Medieval Trade and Technology* (London: Archetype Publications, 1998), 65–79.

Page 40, The first known mention of 'fox-furred' . . .
Samuel Tymms, *Wills and Inventories from the Registers of the Commissary of Bury* (1850)

Page 40, By the beginning of the seventeenth century, fox pelts exported . . .
Lovegrove, *Silent Fields*

Page 40, 'And though he be right guileful . . . in use of medicine'
www.bestiary.ca/beasts/beast179.htm

Page 42, In fact, very few animals were exempt . . . piglets, poultry and lambs.
Lovegrove, *Silent Fields*

Page 42, The head of a fox . . .
Lovegrove, *Silent Fields*

Page 43, 'A Huntsman cometh into the Hall . . . several appointed places'
William Dugdale, *Historical Memorials*, Part 2 (London: 1790)

Page 43, 'at a famous contest held at Dresden . . . tossed to their deaths'
Howard L. Blackmore, *Hunting Weapons* (London: Barrie & Jenkins, 1971)

Page 44, The hunting of all animals remained a hobby of the royals . . .
Pierce Egan, *Book of Sports* (London, 1836)

Page 45, . . . the fox was considered an inferior animal of the chase . . .
Egan, *Book of Sports*

Page 46, . . . in English parishes considered places of 'high control'.
Lovegrove, *Silent Fields*

Page 47, The last record of a fox killed . . .
Lovegrove, *Silent Fields*

Page 47, Hugo Meynell, described by fellow hunter Dick Christian as a . . .
Mandy de Belin, *From the Deer to the Fox* (Hatfield: University of Hertfordshire Press, 2013)

Page 49, DNA analysis suggests . . .
Macdonald, *Running with the Fox*

Page 50, 'If foxes were not preserved for the pleasure of gentlmen . . .'
Lovegrove, *Silent Fields*

Page 50, . . . between 1800 and 1850 the amount of gorse . . .
David W. Macdonald and Paul J. Johnson, 'The impact of sport hunting: a case study', in V. J. Taylor and N. Dunstone (eds), *The Exploitation of Mammal Populations* (Springer Science & Business Media, 2012)

Page 52, Currently there are 186 packs of foxhounds . . .
Masters of Foxhounds Association, www.mfha.org.uk/about-the-mfha/
the-role-of-the-mfha

Page 52, Elsewhere the numbers are lower . . .
Bailey's Hunting Directory, www.bailyshuntingdirectory.com/directory/

Page 53, 'the supreme horse of the world in speed, courage and quality'
Stephen Wilson, 'How We Inherited Hunting', in David James and
Stephen Wilson (eds), *In Praise Of Hunting* (London: Hollis & Carter, 1960)

Page 56, He denounced Freeman as a milksop . . .
Rob Boddice, 'Manliness and the "Morality of Field Sports":
E. A. Freeman and Anthony Trollope, 1869–71', *The Historian*, vol. 70,
no. 1 (2008), pp. 1–29

Page 57, 'Even in the nineteenth century . . . for the special edification
of the Eton boys'
www.henrysalt.co.uk/reformer/blood-sports/the-eton-hare-hunt

Page 58, On a hare hunt near Upton Park . . .
www.henrysalt.co.uk/reformer/blood-sports/the-eton-hare-hunt

Page 61, As public opinion about fur has soured . . .
Wallen, *Fox*

Page 62, 'Hitler banned fox hunting . . .'
David Harrison and Tony Paterson, 'Thanks to Hitler, hunting with
hounds is still verboten', *Daily Telegraph*, 22 September 2002

CHAPTER 2

General information about the fox's biology and behaviour in this chapter
comes mainly from these excellent sources unless otherwise noted:

Stephen Harris and Phil Baker, *Urban Foxes* (Stowmarket: Whittet Books, 2001)
H. G. Lloyd, *The Red Fox* (London: Batsford, 1980)
David Macdonald, *Running with the Fox* (London: Harper Collins, 1989)

Page 72, Near the sea, a fox may also feed . . .
Stephen Harris, *Foxes*, Mammal Society series (Oswestry: Anthony Nelson,
1984)

Page 72, The amount a fox scavenges . . . 35 per cent in the capital'
Stephen Harris and Phil Baker, *Urban Foxes* (Stowmarket: Whittet Books,
2001)

Page 75, The zoologist David Macdonald . . . had a higher pungency.
Macdonald, *Running with the Fox*

Page 75, Food supply also dictates . . . in response to any
transgressions.
Macdonald, *Running with the Fox*

Page 76, . . . 500 kilometres in Sweden . . .
Macdonald, *Running with the Fox*

Page 76, . . . 394 kilometres in the United States.
Lloyd, *The Red Fox*

Page 76, The average fox will travel the breadth of four to six
territories . . . their own social group.
Macdonald, *Running with the Fox*

Page 76, The sacs contain . . . scent that the hounds pick up during a hunt.
Macdonald, *Running with the Fox*

Page 79, When foxes are aggressive . . . and its back again arched.
Macdonald, *Running with the Fox*

Page 80, One of the secrets . . . swift movement and great endurance.
Lloyd, *The Red Fox*

Page 80, It can run up to . . . 13 kilometres per hour.
Macdonald, *Running with the Fox*

Page 81, When eating, say, . . . as David Macdonald describes it.
Macdonald, *Running with the Fox*

Page 81, Foxes also use their vibrissae . . . longer than those of many
other mammals
J. David Henry, *Red Fox: The Catlike Canine* (Washington: Smithsonian Books,
1986)

Page 82, Foxes use scent to locate animals underground . . .
Harris, *Foxes*

Page 83, Between 2008 and 2010 . . . to use these magnetic fields to
hunt prey
rsbl.royalsocietypublishing.org/content/7/3/355

Page 84, Some foxes find bank voles and shrews disgusting . . .
Macdonald, *Running with the Fox*

Page 84, Macdonald writes that . . . uneaten around fox dens.
Macdonald, *Running with the Fox*

Page 84, On the Isle of Mull, where there are no foxes . . .
Macdonald, *Running with the Fox*

Page 85, According to one of the world's leading fox experts . . . a problem for the farmer.
Harris, *Foxes*

Page 88, David Macdonald calculated . . .
Macdonald, *Running with the Fox*

Page 91, The first is called surplus killing . . .
Macdonald, *Running with the Fox*

Page 92, An experiment conducted by David Macdonald . . .
Macdonald, *Running with the Fox*

Page 92, Foxes will cache their food thoroughly . . . tiring work of finding and killing.
Macdonald, *Running with the Fox*

Page 93, He describes the fox 'shaking and licking the flesh . . .
Macdonald, *Running with the Fox*

CHAPTER 3

Page 103, . . . in Bristol up to 37 foxes per square kilometre were recorded . . .
Mike Unwin, *RSPB Spotlight: Foxes* (London: Bloomsbury Natural History, 2015)

Page 103, The population is estimated to be . . .
www.thefoxwebsite.net/foxhunting/huntfoxes

Page 106, The fox's social structure is much more complicated . . . conventional 2.4 family set-up.
Macdonald, *Running with the Fox*

Page 107, Macdonald records watching . . .
Macdonald, *Running with the Fox*

Page 107, In captivity they can reach fourteen to fifteen years . . .
Macdonald, *Running with the Fox*

Page 109, Other sounds include . . .
Macdonald, *Running with the Fox*

Page 115, A study on regional variation . . . to minimise losses of
livestock and game.
Matthew Heydon and Jonathan, Reynolds, 'Fox (Vulpes vulpes)
management in three contrasting regions of Britain, in relation to
agricultural and sporting interests', *Journal of Zoology*, vol. 251 (June 2000),
pp. 237–52

Page 118, At Loddington, the study found that periods of predator
control . . .
www.gwct.org.uk/research/species/mammals/brown-hare/gamekeeping
-and-brown-hare-numbers/ – see Fig. 1

Page 118, 'We are aware that killing predators . . .'
Paul Brown, 'Songbirds gain from lost predators', *Guardian*, 25 June 2002

Page 118, Some scientists believe a third of all bird species . . .
Gerardo Ceballos, Anne H. Ehrlich and Paul R. Ehrlich, *The Annihilation Of
Nature* (Baltimore: Johns Hopkins University Press, 2015)

Page 121, About 80,000 are thought to be shot each year.
www.gwct.org.uk/wildlife/research/mammals/fox/

Page 122, In some of the most jaw-dropping footage . . .
Winterwatch, BBC2, 27 January 2016, www.bbc.co.uk/programmes/
p03gqpjl

Page 123, In the 1990s, an outbreak of mange . . .
Philip Baker, Stephen Harris and Piran White, 'After the Hunt: The
future for foxes in Britain', International Fund for Animal Welfare,
2005,
www.ifaw.org/sites/default/files/IFAW-after-the-hunt.pdf

Page 123, Over the last three decades an oral vaccine . . .
Conrad M. Freuling et al., 'The elimination of fox rabies from Europe',
Philosophical Transactions of the Royal Society B, 24 June 2013, rstb.royalsociety
publishing.org/content/368/1623/20120142

Page 123, According to scientists at Bristol University . . .
www.bristol.ac.uk/biology/research/ecological/vpe/endo/helminth.html

Page 124, Aside from misadventure . . . the population will do so too.
Macdonald, *Running with the Fox*

Page 125, Malcolm Brockless, the gamekeeper employed . . .
Brown, 'Songbirds gain from lost predators'

Page 125, A computer experiment, conducted by Jonathan Reynolds . . .
S. P. Rushton, M. D. F. Shirley, D. W. Macdonald and J. C. Reynolds,
'Effects of Culling Fox Populations at the Landscape Scale: A Spatially
Explicit Population Modeling Approach', *The Journal of Wildlife Management*,
vol. 70, no. 4 (October 2006), pp. 1102–10

Page 125, They found that the most effective way. . . culling foxes did
not work.
http://www.thefoxwebsite.net/foxhunting/huntcontrol

Page 125, Another study, of forests in upland Wales . . .
P. J. Baker and S. Harris, 'Does culling reduce fox (*Vulpes vulpes*) density
in commercial forests in Wales, UK?', *European Journal of Wildlife Research*,
vol. 52, no. 2 (June 2006), pp. 99–108, research-information.bristol
.ac.uk/en/publications/does-culling-reduce-fox-vulpes-vulpes-density
-in-commercial-forests-in-wales-uk(d169d72e-8937-4745-92bf
-fc83ea0beeb4).html

Page 126, It is worth considering, however . . .
Heydon and Reynolds, 'Demography of rural foxes (*Vulpes vulpes*) in
relation to cull intensity'

Page 136, An experiment by David Cowan, Jonathan Reynolds and
Elaine Gill . . .
L. Morris Gosling and William J. Sutherland, *Behaviour and Conservation*
(Cambridge: Cambridge University Press, 2000)

CHAPTER 4

Page 141, George Osbaldeston (1786–1866), known as the 'Squire of
England' . . . and the legend continued.
George Osbaldeston and E. D. Cummings, *Squire Osbaldeston: His Autobiography*
(London: John Lane, 1926)

Page 143, After all, 50,000 hunters signed the 'Hunting Declaration'
Charles Clover, 'Majority vote to defy a Labour ban on hunting', *Telegraph*,
24 July 2004

Page 148, . . . by 2050, it is thought 89 per cent . . .
'World Urbanization Prospects: The 2014 Revison, Highlights', United
Nations, Department of Economic and Social Affairs, 2014, esa.un.org/
unpd/wup/highlights/wup2014-highlights.pdf

Page 150, A report for the National Trust . . .
Patrick Bateson and Elizabeth L. Bradshaw, 'Physiological effects of hunting red deer (*Cervus Elaphus*)', Royal Society Publishing, 1997

Page 151, In 2000, five options were presented . . . with local referendums.
www.theguardian.com/politics/homeaffairs/page/0,,650062,00.html

Page 152, In 2001, MPs backed the total ban on fox hunting . . .
George Jones and Benedict Brogan, 'MPs vote for total ban on hunting', *Daily Telegraph*, 18 January 2001

Page 152, The response to the announcement . . . came into effect on Friday, 18 February 2005.
www.theguardian.com/politics/homeaffairs/page/0,,650062,00.html

Page 153, A MORI poll in 1997 . . .
www.ipsos-mori.com/researchpublications/researcharchive/2153/Hunting-To-Ban-Or-Not-To-Ban.aspx

Page 153, In March 2002 . . .
www.ipsos-mori.com/researchpublications/researcharchive/981/Poll-Shows-Public-Support-For-Ban-On-Hunting.aspx

Page 153, Ten years after the ban . . .
www.ipsos-mori.com/researchpublications/researcharchive/3674/Hunting-Poll-2015.aspx

Page 153, A poll in the same year . . .
www.telegraph.co.uk/news/politics/david-cameron/11454925/David-Cameron-People-should-have-the-freedom-to-hunt.html

Page 153, . . . another, commissioned by the Countryside Alliance . . .
www.countryside-alliance.org/only-40-support-hunt-ban-poll-buries-myth-of-public-support-for-hunting-act/

Page 157, an 'interim measure . . . the infrastructure of hunting'
www.countryside-alliance.org/ca/file/_Revised_Hunting_Handbook_Sept_2005.pdf

Page 158, The League is supportive . . .
www.league.org.uk/our-campaigns/hunting-with-dogs/hunting-facts-and-fiction/hunting-traditions-traditional-drag-or-trail

Page 164, The 'seventeen-hand horses were snorting . . . he had rediscovered his life'.
Roger Scruton, *On Hunting* (London: Yellow Jersey, 1998)

Page 165, In fact, hunting has traditionally been . . . colonial warfare.
Tony Mason and Eliza Riedi, *Sport and the Military: The British Armed Forces 1880–1960* (Cambridge: Cambridge University Press, 2010)

Page 166, Percival Marling . . . a pack of hounds.
Mason and Riedi, *Sport and the Military*

Page 166, . . . Winston Churchill ruled that . . . the British commander Sir John Harding.
Owen Bowcott, 'Churchill reined in army enthusiasm for fox hunts in the Rhine', *Guardian*, 1 August 2010

Page 170, As he puts it: 'As the hounds close in . . . bringing the performance to a conclusion.'
Garry Marvin, 'Natural Instincts and Cultural Passions: Transformations and Performances in Foxhunting', *Performance Research*, vol. 5, no. 2 (2000), pp. 108–15

Page 171, In a pamphlet called 'An introduction to fox hunting' . . .
www.countryside-alliance.org/ca/file/Hunting_for_Kids.pdf

Page 172, They cite instances where video footage . . .
Toni Shephard, Winchester Hunting Symposium, 28 November 2015, www.youtube.com/playlist?list=PLFcSZizooL63hyILbzM9Bflwi2fs0n37s

Page 172, In June 2015, sixteen fox cubs were . . .
www.bbc.co.uk/news/uk-33100242

Page 172, The GWCT study, mentioned in Chapter 3 . . .
Heydon and Reynolds, 'Fox (*Vulpes vulpes*) management in three contrasting regions of Britain'

Page 173, The Countryside Alliance also believes . . . other ways of killing foxes'.
www.countryside-alliance.org/ca/file/Hunting_for_Kids.pdf

Page 176, Those who take part in . . . which other cultures engage.
J. Serpell, *In The Company Of Animals* (Cambridge: Cambridge University Press, 1996)

CHAPTER 5

Page 198, . . . they killed 1,065 otters
Mike Huskisson, *Outfoxed* (London: Michael Huskisson Associates, 1983)

Page 204, In 1975, a slot on the BBC's *Open Door* programme . . .
Dave Wetton, 'Early Days Of The HSA: A personal view', *HOWL*, The Hunt Saboteurs Association, Winter 2013

Page 205, . . . discussing such wide-ranging topics as . . .
Wetton, 'Early Days of the HSA'

Page 206, There was a link between . . . Critics called them terrorists.
Huskisson, *Outfoxed*
Cindy C. Combs and Martin W. Slann, *Encyclopedia of Terrorism*, Revised edition (New York: Facts on File, 2007)
www.animalliberationfront.com

Page 207, ALF activity is now mainly about freeing animals from factory farms
www.indymedia.org.uk/en/2012/09/500050.html

Page 208, Eventually the police suspended . . .
Valerie Elliott, 'Fury as police drop probe . . .', *Daily Mail*, 18 April 2015

Page 208, Tim Bonner of the Countryside Alliance . . .
'Campaign to unmask violent anti-hunt protesters is stepped up after attackers go unpunished', *Western Morning News*, 19 April 2015

Page 208, In January 2016, a family of three sabbing . . .
stv.tv/news/tayside/1340621-fox-hunt-protester-family-fined-after
-taking-their-own-film-to-police/

Page 211, In January 2016, four police in Lincolnshire . . .
www.lincs.police.uk/news-campaigns/news/2016op-galileo
-enforcement-update/

CHAPTER 6

Page 228, 'We explained to him [Romeo] . . .
www.bbc.co.uk/news/uk-england-london-12573364

Page 228, In the late 1950s, the Natural History Society recorded . . .
Harris and Baker, *Urban Foxes*

Page 229, although this expansion was checked . . .
Baker, Harris and White, 'After the Hunt'

Page 229, The overall population is thought to have been stable at 33,000 . . .
Harris and Yalden (eds), *Mammals of the British Isles Handbook*

Page 229, The fox is relatively small . . . from garden sheds to roofs.
Harris, *Foxes*

Page 229, It is said that there are more than 10,000 foxes . . .
Sarah Knapton, 'Londoners call in snipers to shoot dangerous urban
foxes', *Telegraph*, 8 December 2014

Page 230, A study in Bristol suggested . . .
www.thefoxwebsite.net/urbanfoxes/urbandiet

Page 230, 'degree of ecological plasticity was unparalleled for a
carnivore of this size'.
Macdonald, *Running with the Foxes*

Page 230, Two fox experts . . . into the built-up centres of our cities.
Harris and Baker, *Urban Foxes*

Page 233, Harris, who has studied urban foxes for decades . . . often
mistaken for mange.
Harris and Baker, *Urban Foxes*

Page 235, Of 1,225 pet cats, eight had been killed . . .
Harris and Baker, *Urban Foxes*

Page 237, 'I'm absolutely convinced . . .'
news.bbc.co.uk/1/hi/uk/england/2078419.stm

Page 239, These incidents are all labelled . . . these occasions have been
very rare.
Stephen Harris, 'Can we live with foxes?', *BBC Wildlife*, Summer 2013

Page 239, According to the Office for National Statistics . . . the victims
are often young children.
Haroon Siddique, 'Hospital admissions for injuries caused by dogs
up 76% in 10 years', *Guardian*, 28 May 2015, and blogs.channel4.com/
factcheck/factcheck-qa-facts-dog-attacks/17727

Page 243, Another reason why foxes . . . call in pest controllers with a
rifle.
Harris, 'Can we live with foxes?'

Page 244, The club was in the news in 2015 . . . pinned in a child's
playground
Graeme Brown, 'Eight people outfoxed as bushy tailed bully keeps them
trapped in a club' *Mirror*, 1 July 2015
Lucy Crossley, 'Fox terrifies club drinkers . . .', *Mail*, 2 July 2015

'"Vicious" fox traps eight people in Cambridgeshire sports club', BBC News, 2 July 2015

Page 247, An ITN video package . . .
www.telegraph.co.uk/news/earth/wildlife/11923915/Council-scraps-urban -fox-cull-in-face-of-protests.html

Page 248, A fox was 'skulking in the shadows . . . narrowly escaped death'.
Giles Sheldrick, 'Boy just seconds away from fox horror in bedroom', *Express*, 28 October 2011

Page 250, (6.5 kilograms for a fully grown dog fox . . . just under 10 kilograms
Harris and Baker, *Urban Foxes*

Page 250, 'We are not seeing urban foxes get any bigger'
http://www.bbc.co.uk/nature/17270249

Page 250, One factor that can affect size . . . titbits brought home by mother.
Harris, 'Can we live with foxes?', *BBC Wildlife*

Page 254, . . . 86 per cent of city-dwellers like foxes . . . enriches their lives.
www.channel4.com/info/press/news/foxes-live-wild-in-the-city -survey-results

Page 259, . . . about two-thirds of the area is ancient woodland.
www.highweald.org/downloads/publications/land-management-guidance/ woodland-guidance/1145-woodlands-in-the-weald-habitat-leaflet/file .html

Page 265, Gus the Fox is a kind of absurdist parody . . . punching swans.
Matt Haydock, *Gus the Fox: A scrapbook* (London: Short Books, 2013)

Page 270, Chris once told the *Evening Standard* . . .
Mark Blunden, 'Chris Packham: It's OK to feed urban Foxes', *Evening Standard*, 7 October 2013, www.standard.co.uk/news/uk/chris-packham -its-ok-to-feed-urban-foxes-8863724.html

Bibliography

Anon., *Sir Gawain and the Green Knight* (c. 14th century)

Baker, P. J., and Harris, S., 'Does culling reduce fox (*Vulpes vulpes*) density in commercial forests in Wales, UK?', *European Journal of Wildlife Research*, vol. 52, no. 2 (June 2006)

Barkham, Patrick, *Badgerlands* (London: Granta Books, 2013)

Baxter, I. L., and Hamilton-Dyer, S., 'Foxy in furs?', *Archaeofauna*, vol. 12, 2003

Beckford, Peter, *Thoughts on Hunting* (London: Hodder & Stoughton, 1911)

de Belin, Mandy, *From the Deer to the Fox* (Hatfield: University of Hertfordshire Press, 2013)

Blackmore, Howard L., *Hunting Weapons* (London: Barrie & Jenkins, 1971)

Blair, Tony, *A Journey: My Political Life* (London: Hutchinson, 2010)

Blome, Richard, and Cox, Nicholas, *The Gentleman's Recreation* (London: S. Roycroft for Richard Blome, 1686)

Boddice, Rob, 'Manliness and the "Morality of Field Sports": E. A. Freeman and Anthony Trollope, 1869–71', *The Historian*, vol. 70, no. 1 (2008)

Burrows, Roger, *Wild Fox* (Newton Abbott: David & Charles, 1968)

Cameron, Esther (ed.), *Leather and Fur: Aspects of Early Medieval Trade and Technology* (London: Archetype Publications, 1998)

Carr, Raymond, *English Foxhunting: A History* (London: Weidenfeld and Nicolson, 1976)

Caxton, William (trans.), *The History of Reynard The Fox* (1481)

Ceballos, Gerardo, Ehrlich, Anne H., and Ehrlich, Paul R., *The Annihilation Of Nature* (Baltimore: Johns Hopkins University Press, 2015)

Celoria, Francis (trans.), *The Metamorphoses Of Antoninus Liberalis* (London: Routledge, 1992)

Cockaine, Thomas, 'A Short Treatise of Hunting' (1591)

Combs, Cindy C., and Slann, Martin W., *Encyclopedia of Terrorism*, Revised edition (New York: Facts on File, 2007)

Cook, John, *Observations on Fox Hunting* (1826)

Cosslett, Tess, *Talking Animals in British Children's Fiction* (London: Ashgate Publishing, 2006)

Creswell, Richard (trans.), *Aristotle's History Of Animals* (London: Henry G. Bohn, 1862)

Dahl, Roald, *Fantastic Mr Fox* (London: George Allen & Unwin, 1970)

Dahl, Roald, *The Magic Finger* (London: George Allen & Unwin, 1968)

Dahl, Roald, *My Year* (London: Jonathan Cape, 1993)

Dann, Colin, *Animals of Farthing Wood* (London: Heinemann, 1979)

Dugdale, William, *Historical Memorials*, Part 2 (London: 1790)

Eder, K., *The Social Construction of Nature* (London: Sage Publications, 1996)

Egan, Pierce, *Book of Sports* (London, 1836)

Freethy, Ron, *Man and Beast: The Natural and Unnatural History of British Mammals* (London: Blandford Press, 1984)

Freuling, Conrad M., et al., 'The elimination of fox rabies from Europe', *Philosophical Transactions of the Royal Society B*, 24 June 2013

Gosling, L. Morris, and Sutherland, William J., *Behaviour and Conservation* (Cambridge: Cambridge University Press, 2000)

Harris, Stephen, *Foxes*, Mammal Society series (Oswestry: Anthony Nelson, 1984)

Harris, Stephen, and Baker, Phil, *Urban Foxes* (Stowmarket: Whittet Books, 2001)

Harris, Stephen, and Yalden, Derek (eds), *Mammals of the British Isles Handbook* (Southampton: The Mammal Society, 2008)

Haydock, Matt, *Gus the Fox: A scrapbook* (London: Short Books, 2013)

Hemmington, Martin, *Foxwatching* (Stowmarket: Whittet Books, 1997)

Henry, J. David, *Red Fox: The Catlike Canine* (Washington: Smithsonian Books, 1986)

Heydon, Matthew, and Reynolds, Jonathan, 'Demography of rural foxes (*Vulpes vulpes*) in relation to cull intensity in three contrasting regions of Britain', *Journal of Zoology*, vol. 251 (June 2000)

Heydon, Matthew, and Reynolds, Jonathan, 'Fox (Vulpes vulpes) management in three contrasting regions of Britain, in relation to agricultural and sporting interests', *Journal of Zoology*, vol. 251 (June 2000)

Holmes-Walker, Anthony, *Sixes and Sevens: A Short History of the Skinners' Company* (London: The Skinners' Company, 2005)

Howard-Johnston, James, 'Trading in fur from classical antiquity to the early middle ages', in E. Cameron, *Leather and Fur. Aspects of Early Medieval Trade and Technology* (London: Archetype Publications, 1998)

Huskisson, Mike, *Outfoxed* (London: Michael Huskisson Associates, 1983)

James, David, and Wilson, Stephen (eds), *In Praise Of Hunting* (London: Hollis & Carter, 1960)

Kurtén, Björn, *Pleistocene Mammals of Europe* (Piscataway: Transaction Publishers, 1968)

Leopold, Aldo, *A Sand County Almanac* (New York: Ballantine Books, 1970)

Lloyd, H. G., *The Red Fox* (London: Batsford, 1980)

Lopez, Barry, *Arctic Dreams* (London: Picador, 1987)

Lovegrove, Roger, *Silent Fields* (Oxford: Oxford University Press, 2007)

Lydekker, Richard, *A Geographical History of Mammals* (Cambridge: Cambridge University Press, 1896)

Macdonald, David, *Running with the Fox* (London, Harper Collins, 1989)

Macdonald, David, and Feber, Ruth, *Wildlife Conservation On Farmland*, vols I and 2 (Oxford: Oxford University Press, 2015)

Macdonald, David W., and Johnson, Paul J., 'The impact of sport hunting: a case study', in V. J. Taylor and N. Dunstone (eds), *The Exploitation of Mammal Populations* (Springer Science & Business Media, 2012)

Marks, Richard, *Stained Glass in England During the Middle Ages* (London: Routledge, 1993)

Marvin, Garry, 'Natural Instincts and Cultural Passions: Transformations and Performances in Foxhunting', *Performance Research*, vol. 5, no. 2 (2000)

Mason, Tony, and Riedi, Eliza, *Sport and the Military: The British Armed Forces 1880–1960* (Cambridge: Cambridge University Press, 2010)

Maurel, Daniel, et al., 'Seasonal moulting patterns in three fur bearing mammals' *Canadian Journal of Zoology*, vol. 64, no. 8 (1986)

May, Allyson N., *The Fox-Hunting Controversy, 1781–2004* (Farnham: Ashgate, 2003)

Osbaldeston, George, and Cummings, E. D., *Squire Osbaldeston: His Autobiography* (London: John Lane, 1926)

Potter, Beatrix, *Mr Tod* (London: Frederick Warne & Co., 1912)

Pye-Smith, Charlie, *The Facts Of Rural Life* (London: Veterinary Association for Wildlife Management, 2015)

Pye-Smith, Charlie, *Fox Hunting: Beyond The Propaganda* (Wildlife Network, 1997)

Pye-Smith, Charlie, *Rural Rites: Hunting and the Politics of Prejudice* (London: Middle Way Group, 2006)

Ridley, Jane, *Fox Hunting* (London: Harper Collins, 1990)

Roberts, Charles G. D., *Red Fox* (Boston: L. C. Page and Company, 1910)

Rushton, S. P., Shirley, M. D. F., Macdonald, D. W., and Reynolds, J. C., 'Effects of Culling Fox Populations at the Landscape Scale: A Spatially Explicit Population Modeling Approach', *The Journal of Wildlife Management*, vol. 70, no. 4 (October 2006)

Reynolds, Jonathan, C., *Fox Control in the Countryside* (Game Conservancy, 2000)

de Saint-Exupéry, Antoine, *The Little Prince* (New York: Reynal & Hitchcock, 1943)

Salt, Henry, (ed.), *Killing For Sport* (London: G. Bell and Sons, 1914)

Salt, Henry, *Seventy Years Among Savages* (London: Allen and Unwin, 1921)

Sassoon, Siegfried, *Memoirs Of A Fox-Hunting Man* (London: Faber and Faber, 1928)

Scruton, Roger, *On Hunting* (London: Yellow Jersey, 1998)

Serpell, J., *In The Company Of Animals* (Cambridge: Cambridge University Press, 1996)

Sherman, Josepha (ed.), *Storytelling: An Encyclopedia of Mythology and Folklore* (New York: M. E. Sharpe, 2008)

Simpson, James (trans.), *Reynard The Fox* (New York: Liveright Publishing Corporation, 2015)

Smith, Julie A., and Mitchell, Robert W. (eds), *Experiencing Animal Minds: An Anthology Of Animal-Human Encounters* (New York: Columbia University Press, 2012)

Smith, Thomas, *Extracts from the Diary Of A Huntsman* (London: Edward Arnold & Co., 1921)

Smith, Thomas, *The Life Of A Fox, Written By Himself* (London: Whittaker and Co., 1843)

Smyers, Karen Ann, *The Fox and the Jewel* (Honolulu: University of Hawai'i Press, 1998)

Solnit, Rebecca, *Wanderlust* (London: Granta Books, 2014)

Stoutenburg, Adrien, *Short History of the Fur Trade* (London: Andre Deutsch, 1970)

Sturrock, Donald, *Storyteller: The Authorized Biography of Roald Dahl* (London: Simon & Schuster, 2010)

Thompson, John A., *Fox Hunting: The Damage Committee and other sporting history in Dumfriesshire* (privately published, 2010)

Tickner, John, *Tickner's Hunting Field* (New York: Putnam, 1970)

Topsell, Edward, *The History of Four-footed Beasts and Serpents* (1658)

Travers, P. L., *Mary Poppins* (London: Harper Collins, 1934)

Tremain, Ruthven, *The Animal's Who's Who* (New York: Scribner, 1984)

Turberville, George, *The Noble Arte of Venerie or Hunting* (1576)

Unwin, Mike, *RSPB Spotlight: Foxes* (London: Bloomsbury Natural History, 2015)

Varty, Kenneth, *Reynard, Renart, Reinaert and Other Foxes in Medieval England* (Amsterdam: Amsterdam University Press, 1999)

Veale, Elspeth Mary, *The English Fur Trade in the Later Middle Ages* (Oxford: Clarendon Press, 1966)

Vesey-Fitzgerald, Brian, *Town Fox, Country Fox* (London: Andre Deutsch, 1965)

Wallen, Martin, *Fox* (London: Reaktion Books, 2006)

Watson, Frederick, *Hunting Pie* (London: H. F. & G. Witherby, 1931)

White, T. H., *The Book of Beasts* (Madison: Parallel Press, 2002)

Williams, Trevor, and Bryant, John, *Unearthing The Urban Fox* (Herne Bay: Foxolutions Publishing, 2012)

Woods, Michael, 'Fantastic Mr Fox? Representing Animals in the Hunting Debate', in Philo, Chris, and Wilbert, Chris (eds), *Animal Spaces, Beastly Places: New Geographies of Human–Animal Relations* (London: Routledge, 2000)

'World Urbanization Prospects: The 2014 Revison, Highlights', United Nations, Department of Economic and Social Affairs (2014)

Wright, Thomas, *Popular Treatises on Science Written During the Middle Ages* (London, 1741)

Xenophon, *Cynegeticus* [Hunting with Dogs] (c. 4th century BC)

Yalden, Derek, *The History of British Mammals* (Cambridge: Academic Press, 2002)

MAGAZINES AND NEWSPAPERS

BBC Wildlife magazines

HOWL magazines

New Yorker magazines

Daily Mail archive

Daily Telegraph archive

Evening Standard archive
Express archive
Guardian archive
Mirror archive

WEBSITES

www.animalliberationfront.com
www.bailyshuntingdirectory.com
www.channel4.com
www.countryside-alliance.org
www.gwct.org.uk
www.henrysalt.co.uk
www.highweald.org
www.indymedia.org.uk
www.ipsos-mori.com
www.league.org.uk
www.mfha.org.uk
www.thefoxwebsite.net

Acknowledgements

This book is very much a product of people being generous with their time – and I have many to thank. I am exceedingly grateful to those who spoke, met, corresponded with or hosted me, with special thanks to: Brian Fanshawe, Charlie Pye-Smith, Rebecca Hosking, Brian May, Chris Packham, Alastair Leake, Louis Masai Michel, Nicholas Newton-Fisher, Sandra Reddy, Bruce Lindsay-Smith, Ricky Gervais, Andrew Cook, Trevor Williams, Graham Hirons, Roger Scruton, Gwyn Williams, Michael Thompson, Garry Marvin, Alfie Moon, Dave Wetton, Simon Russell, John Prestige, Jim Barrington, Rachel White, Dominic Gregory, Colin Race, Matt Haydock, Anatoly Liberman, Dawn Scott, Don Gutoski, Richard Bowler and Jessica Groling.

Plenty of others gave me their time, knowledge, thoughts, contacts and experience. I especially thank Eamonn Lawlor, Jasmine Allen, Toni Shephard, Andy Richardson, Alison Sealey, Chris Pak and Dominic Dyer. I also thank Faith and Clive Sinclair, Brenda and Diarmuid Clohessy, Robert Maitland, Rory and Matt, and Ben Hoare at *BBC Wildlife* magazine for aiding my research. And the many friends who sent me foxy links, books, videos, photos, news stories and accounts of their own sightings.

I could not have written a book about foxes without drawing on the excellent work of David Macdonald and Stephen Harris, who have studied *Vulpes vulpes* more than any other scientists in the world. I am indebted to their many decades of superb research. I am also incredibly grateful for the generous support of the Society of Authors' Authors' Foundation for the Award in memory of the late, great Roger Deakin, which enabled me to write the book.

I am extremely grateful to Jennie Condell, publisher at Elliott & Thompson, who commissioned me to write *Foxes Unearthed*, and Pippa Crane, senior editor at Elliott & Thompson, for their dedication, passion, diligence, insight and support throughout the whole process. I also thank the wider team at E&T: Lorne Forsyth, Marianne Thorndahl, Jill Burrows, Matt Adam Williams, Alison Menzies, Ollie Dewis, Tim Oakenfull for the beautiful illustrations and Nathan Burton for the stunning book cover.

Finally, I thank my family. My grandmother Shirley, for talking to me about Grandpa, and for passing on a love of nature. My grandmother Barbara, for passing on a love of books and reading. To my parents, Mark and Philippa, and Ed and Len, for their support and encouragement. And, Jim, for everything.

Index

Index

ABOUT THE AUTHOR

Lucy Jones is a writer and journalist based in Hampshire, England. She previously worked at *NME* and the *The Daily Telegraph*. Her writing on culture, science and nature has been published in *BBC Earth*, *BBC Wildlife*, the *Guardian*, *TIME*, *Newsweek* and the *New Statesman*. She runs the Wildlife Daily blog and is the recipient of the Society of Authors' Roger Deakin Award for *Foxes Unearthed*.